SOUVENIR OF FLORIDA & CUBA 1886

**PUBLICATIONS OF THE SOCIETY OF SPANISH
AND SPANISH-AMERICAN STUDIES**

Luis T. González-del-Valle, *Director*

ROGER WILLIAMS WOODBURY

SOUVENIR OF FLORIDA & CUBA 1886

Edited with an
introduction by
Luis T. González-del-Valle

SOCIETY OF SPANISH AND SPANISH-AMERICAN STUDIES

© Copyright, Society of Spanish and Spanish-American Studies, 2005.

All rights reserved. No portion of this book may be reproduced, by any process or technique, without the express written consent of the publisher. The book may be quoted as part of scholarly studies.

The Society of Spanish and Spanish-American Studies promotes bibliographical, critical and pedagogical research in Spanish and Spanish-American studies by publishing works of particular merit in these areas. On occasion, the Society also publishes creative works. SSSAS is a non-profit educational organization sponsored by the University of Colorado at Boulder. It is located in the Department of Spanish and Portuguese, University of Colorado, UCB 278, Boulder, Colorado, 80309-0278. U.S.A.

International Standard Book Number (ISBN): 0-89295-119-2.

Library of Congress Control Number: 2005931225.

Printed in the United States of America.
Impreso en los Estados Unidos de América.

This text was prepared for publication by
Adler Enterprises LLC, Lafayette, Colorado.

CONTENTS

Introduction. Luis T. González-del-Valle ix
Preface 3
Cincinnati to Jacksonville 9
Jacksonville 18
Jacksonville to Tampa 26
Tampa 30
The Gulf of Mexico 35
First Glimpses of Havana 43
Hotel Life 48
On the San Carlos Roof 60
Letters of Introduction 63
Street Scenes 66
Modes of Travel 71
Talking Spanish 74
Markets and Restaurants 77
Dinero 80
Theatres, Clubs and Music 88
The Churches 93
The Forts 100
The Weed 106
The Royal Lottery 109
The Cock Pit 113
Plaza de Toros 116
Neighboring Towns 127
Miscellaneous Havana Incidents 132
Matanzas 136
Preparing for Departure 144
Havana to Tampa 146
Tampa Again 149
Manatee and Gators 152
Tampa to St. Augustine 157
St. Augustine 160
Homeward Bound 164

APPENDICES
Chronological 165
Chief Expenses 167
Cribbage 168

CONCLUDING ILLUSTRATIONS
Roger Williams Woodbury 169
Manuscript Sample 170
Map of Havana 173
Map of Cuba 174

To the Regents: the men and women who unselfishly have served the University and the people of Colorado for so many years.

INTRODUCTION

On Wednesday, December 30, 1885, Mr. Roger Williams Woodbury and his wife, Anna, began a journey from Denver to Florida and Cuba, venturing through Kansas, Missouri, Ohio, Tennessee, and Georgia. In Cincinnati, they met another couple, Mike and Jane, Colorado friends who several weeks earlier had decided to join them in their exploration of the Caribbean. Thus, just over two decades after the end of the American Civil War, a Yankee (Roger) and a Southerner (Mike), embarked on a spontaneous adventure. Despite their lingering memories of the most dramatic military and social conflict in United States history, the two men carried on amicably during the ten weeks they shared.

The end result of their voyage was a third-person narrative of their travel endeavors. Although not clearly identified as its author, in all probability Roger Woodbury was responsible for drafting this text, an inference justified by virtue of his background as a newspaperman and the similarities between his penmanship and the calligraphy used throughout the manuscript. In addition, the frequent usage of the masculine pronoun in reference to the tale's author indicates our narrator is a man. Finally, Roger is clearly the manuscript's protagonist: his name appears one hundred and seventy-two times. His closest rival is Mike with one hundred and thirty-five references, whereas Anna attracts thirty-five and Jane eighteen. The consistent reference to Roger is eminently logical in an autobiographical travel account such as the one we are about to reproduce. In order to maintain the verisimilitude required in tales of this nature, one must have firsthand knowledge of what transpired. We learn with certainty from the book's preface that Roger suggested a trip to Cuba with two former travel companions who had accompanied him to California during the winter of 1884. This journey resulted in an "anonymous but standard volume of travel entitled *A Souvenir of California*," one we are told —in the humorous fashion which prevails throughout the tale— "rapidly ran through an edition of three volumes." Thus, with this remark the narrator indicates that the previous account had remained virtually unknown to all but the three gentlemen who visited California in 1884, a situation which until now has coincided with the fate afforded the text that follows this introduction (namely, *Souvenir of Florida & Cuba 1886*).

About the Author

The fifth child of Henry Woodbury and Hannah Davidson Woodbury, Roger Williams Woodbury was born in Francestown, New Hampshire, on March 3, 1841.[1] Prone to illness from childhood, young Roger came from a family lacking financial resources. His father had been a farmer and a bootmaker. Roger received hand-me-downs from an older brother. Eventually he and his siblings had to enter the work force in order to supplement the family income. The scarcity of financial resources confronted by Roger during his early years may explain his tightness with money during his trip to Florida and Cuba in 1886, a fact he openly and humoristically acknowledges.

In typical 19th century New England fashion, the family did not lack religious faith, and thus provided Roger with a Protestant upbringing. His early schooling took place in his hometown and continued when the family moved to Manchester. As an active and educated urban dweller in this region of the United States,[2] he joined several cultural societies popular with young adults during those years.[3] At age twelve, for example, he formed a debating society, a group instrumental in developing the administrative skills which would become essential to the well-being of his business undertakings in Denver years later. Soon after, he joined The Band of Hope, a temperance society, and became a member of the Young Men's Republican Club of Manchester between 1852 and 1856 (in this group, once again, he attained the title of Secretary). At age 16, he joined the Excelsior Literary Association, a membership he continued until his first marriage.[4] In the *Manuscript Biography of RWW*, we learn that from early on he also demonstrated an affinity for books and correspondence.

While in Manchester, Mr. Woodbury became a printer and, in 1859, began working for the *Daily Mirror* as an apprentice, where he pursued numerous other assignments and eventually became an editor. Here, his activities in the areas of printing and journalism would prove beneficial for his future ventures in Denver. About the time he joined the *Daily Mirror*, he married a former classmate he had remained acquainted with for a number of years.[5] His new wife, Emma J. York, was one-and-a-half years younger than him. According to Mr. Woodbury, this union had "unfortunate aspects," aspects which he never reveals (*Manuscript Biography*). During his first marriage, Roger had a son named Frank who was born in New Hampshire, in 1861.[6]

While in New Hampshire, Roger Woodbury was fortunate to hear a speech by Abraham Lincoln before he ascended to the presidency of the United States. Soon after, when then-President Lincoln called for volunteers after the fall of Fort Sumter, Roger enlisted in Company A of the Third New Hampshire Infantry. His rich experiences during the Civil War were discussed at length in volume three of the *Manuscript Biography*, including information on his participation in a Florida campaign during 1864 near Jacksonville and other northern areas of the state (pp. 255-79).[7]

On August 2, 1865, after the "War of the Rebellion" had concluded, Mr. Woodbury returned to Manchester, where he remained until April 19, 1866, when he left New Hampshire for Colorado. During his nine months in Manchester, he became a mason, was involved with the printing of a book and, once again, became a reporter for the *Daily Mirror*. On his way to Colorado, he visited his father in Leavenworth, Kansas and finally arrived in Denver on May 15, 1866 and subsequently became a prospector. After a less than successful first season prospecting in the Rockies, he returned to Denver, where he began working for the *Daily Rocky Mountain News*.[8] Soon after, in March, 1867, he accepted a position with the *Denver Daily*, a newspaper owned by Mr. L. M. Koons[9] (the paper almost immediately changed its title to the *Daily Colorado Tribune* and later, in 1871, became the *Denver Tribune*). During the fall of 1867, Roger Woodbury became one of its owners and employed his influence to advocate for the development of rail service. By the end of 1871, he had sold his interest in the *Daily Colorado Tribune*.[10] Soon after, he purchased the *Denver Daily Times*, a Republican newspaper he maintained until 1882, when he sold it to his son Frank. Throughout his life, Mr. Woodbury owned or co-owned numerous newspapers in Denver (both dailies and weeklies). Their titles and dates often overlapped. It is difficult to distinguish between them over a century later (frequently, these were ephemeral publications that are extremely hard to locate at present).

On July 28, 1870, Mr. Woodbury was remarried to Mrs. Anna Koons, the widow of Mr. L. M. Koons.[11] In the early 1880s, he became the President of the Denver Chamber of Commerce and Board of Trade. As reported in the December 31, 1885 issue of the *Rocky Mountain News* and in the *Souvenir of Florida*, on December 30th he was given $1,000 by the Board of Directors of this organization in appreciation for his prior services. On this same day, he and his wife Anna began their Florida and Cuba-bound expedition, a trip that concluded on March 13, 1886. Soon after, he acquired a controlling interest and functioned as President of the Union Bank of Denver, where he remained until the Panic of 1893. During the late 1890s, he was President of the California-Eastern Railway Company and President of the Cochiti Reduction and Improvement Company of Denver which operated a mill in

New Mexico. With such an impressive resumé, we can conclude that beyond his involvement with the Chamber, Mr. Woodbury's influence was felt in numerous ways in Colorado. In addition to the achievements already mentioned, he was also instrumental in the establishment of the first free public library in Denver and Colorado[12] and of the Denver Clearing House Association; he was —with twenty-eight others— an incorporator of the State Historical Society of Colorado and held various significant positions with the Masons. Governor F. W. Pitking appointed him Brigadier General of the Colorado National Guard, where he served on the executive staff. Lastly, he was elected Regent of the University of Colorado. He served in the Board of Regents from 1884 to 1890. In 1890, a new building —a men's dormitory— was named in his honor; it currently houses parts of the College of Arts and Sciences.

Since his arrival to Colorado, Mr. Roger W. Woodbury undoubtedly was heavily involved with industries associated with power, prestige and wealth during the second half of the 19th century in the United States (namely, banking, rail transportation, and newspapers). Although he did not possess the same economic standing and notoriety of some other post-Civil War contemporaries (i.e., John D. Rockefeller, Andrew Carnegie, Jay Gould, and J. P. Morgan), in the context of Denver, he was a local powerhouse among the empire builders of his age as evidenced, in part, by the magnificent house he built for his family. E. E. Kohl refers to the home built in North Denver as the "most conspicuous mansion on those bluffs across the river" (86). It was finished in 1890 at a cost of $250,000 (89). Kohl describes it as follows:

> The Woodbury place became a landmark; it could be seen for miles around and from its commanding position one had full view of the country and the mountains... The ... Woodbury mansion ... stood secluded in the grove that had grown up within the granite walls. It is a museum in itself. The beautiful Tiffany window in the dining room casts its rich amber light over the .... Belgium rug and a matching Tiffany transom above the front door gives a soft color to the carved oak hall and stairway. (90-91)[13]

As was the case with some of his more prosperous counterparts, Mr. Woodbury was an investor, a shrewd businessman, a promoter, an able manager involved with industries fundamental to the growth and well-being of the rapidly expanding nation, and a philanthropist.[14] After a life of great societal, political and entrepreneurial achievements, Roger Williams Woodbury died of a heart attack in 1903.[15]

As a final consideration on Roger and Anna Woodbury, the two were typical members of the Protestant upper class in America during the last quarter of the 19th century, considered educated in view of the prevailing standards of the time. As Daniel Walker Howe indicates in another context, they were not just Americans, but also Victorians, and American-Victorian culture was "Anglo-Saxon and Protestant" (9); "was bourgeois in origin" (9) and "cosmopolitan in outlook, increasingly self-assertive, expressing its collective pride in literary and philanthropic organizations" (10). Northerners were heavily represented among American-Victorians, "mostly Whig-Republican, literary men and women" who valued "social responsibility, strict personal morality, and respect for cultural standards. They thought of themselves as preserving certain patrician values while democratizing their application" (12). Moreover, they favored "rational order" (18), were thrifty (19) and often "expressed themselves in moral terms" (27).[16] When comparing their displacement practices to those of their ancestors, traveling to them was less of a dangerous adventure. As a result of their expanded leisure time, American-Victorians were fond of vacations facilitated by modern transport (i.e., steamship, railroad).[17]

Souvenir of Florida & Cuba 1886 and its Content

Roger Woodbury's narrative is divided into three distinct parts: travel from Denver to Florida, visit to the Sunshine state (occurring prior and after their Cuban visit), and the Cuban experience. A unifying element throughout the tale is the sense of humor and playfulness he demonstrates. In this vein, we have Roger's encounter with Mike in Cincinnati:

> ... it was with considerable gratification that the two wanderers [i.e., Anna and Roger] through the long depot beheld Mike at the gate with an anxious cast of countenance, chewing upon some astounding Spanish phrase, with which he might welcome them, and at the same time assume the leading position as interpreter. "Buenos Di<u>os</u>," exclaimed he, with outstretched hands and a thrill of pride, to which Roger heartily responded with "Yo estoy un mentiroso." Anna experienced a glow of intense satisfaction at being associated with men who could so readily converse in a foreign tongue,

while the hackmen, thinking they were nothing less than foreign Counts, and therefore unacquainted with schedule prices, rushed upon them with blended looks of hope and anxiety. But when Roger and Anna entered a fifty-cent 'bus, and Mike started away on foot, they gazed after them with unspeakable disgust. ("Cincinnati to Jacksonville")

This anecdote reveals Roger's ability to laugh at himself and his companions, as he playfully satirizes both men's misuse of Spanish,[18] Anna's apparent satisfaction regarding their command of the language, and the resulting reaction of the onlookers. This type of humor, which is sprinkled throughout the tale, attests to the desired objectivity of a narrator whose propensity for laughter demonstrates his capacity to discern the true nature of his travel ventures.[19]

Perhaps the most significant information shared during the Woodburys' journey to Florida concerns Roger's memories and accompanying views regarding the Civil War: over twenty years after the conflict's end, its profound impact on the American consciousness remains detectable in his observations.

The sections of the book devoted to Florida richly detail the daily life of various cities (including Jacksonville, Tampa, St. Augustine and Key West), transportation within the peninsula, its landscape, and certain prevailing pastimes. Both Anna and Roger are able to make comparisons between their experiences in 1886 and those from a prior visit seven years earlier. (In Roger's case, he also draws from his stay as a soldier during the Civil War.) Their contrasts provide a sense of evolvement which should prove useful to students of Floridian history.

Regarding historical and cultural perspectives, their stay in Cuba is undoubtedly the most valuable aspect of this volume. Cuba, after all, was alien to all four visitors, and thus we learn of their initial reactions to the country.[20] As can be expected, a work like *Souvenir* offers a wealth of information on the geography, history, architecture, customs, flora and fauna, and culture of Havana. In this fashion, we witness descriptions of Cuban lifestyle, such as architecture, experiences in a typical hotel (the San Carlos), the predominant modes of transportation (victorias and *volantas*), the people (including the upper classes, beggars, street peddlers, horse bathers, guards), and the food. In addition, we learn about national turmoils such as the longing in Cuba for freedom and the perception by some that the answer to this wish lay with the United States. Moreover, we gain insight on the cruelty towards animals exhibited by some, racial segregation, the internal arrangement of markets, the prices charged for goods and services, etc.

More detailed are the descriptions of the Tacón Theater, the Royal Lottery's functioning and its impact on the population, the nature of cock and bullfights (this last practice was abandoned in Cuba and, therefore, not that much is known about it).

At times, judgments are made on aspects of Cuban life which manifest a profound sense of superiority on the part of the visitors (including the narrator). Thus, we are told that

> Softly treading along the tiles were cats—which with cocks and dogs seemed as natural to Cuban soil as darkeys and fleas. ("On the San Carlos Roof")

> The party never wondered at the low tone of morals in Cuba, and they could not but believe the Church responsible for it. It was said that during Lenten season a notice like the following was always made public: "... His Extremely Illustrious Excellency, Señor Bishop Diocesan, makes known to all and each one of the faithful that goes to hear the word of God in this holy season, that he concedes to them forty days of indulgence for each time that they thus do so; and also, as special apostolic favor, a full indulgence to those that attend four sermons in said missions, and confess and worship devoutly," etc. It was the opinion of the party that the island needed the infusion of a religion which would teach people to think and reason on religious and moral matters for themselves, and not leave it exclusively to the priests; and that the missionary societies of America could do no better work in Asia than in Cuba. ("The Churches")

> The power of Spain seemed to be concentrated mainly at the Capital, and there it was the most needed. If the people grumbled at the expense, they could appropriately remember that their sports, immoralities and natural deviltry made the presence of many guards a necessity. He who dances must pay for the fiddler. ("The Forts")

In all three instances, the views expressed are symptomatic of a sense of superiority assumed by the visitors (including the narrator). Their perceptions illustrate aspects of the concept of Orientalism as coined by Edward Said years later. According to the famous Palestinian, the Orient was not only the origin of European languages and cultures, but also constituted a widely-studied image of the European conception of the "other." The application of this concept is often found in travel books, in which Europeans traveling abroad may project an image of otherness on alien realities, hence distinguishing themselves from the foreign culture and revealing aspects of their own identity.[21] In the specific case of Cuba, the foreigners whose travel experiences are narrated in *Souvenir* deem themselves superior to the locals and, consequently, blame the Catholic Church in Havana for the "low tone of morals." The four visitors conclude that the Cuban people would benefit from religion "which would teach people to think and reason . . . for themselves," or, in other words, that they should imitate American religious values. Similarly, the presence of travelers justifies the abundance of policemen in Havana in view of the prevailing Cuban "immoralities" and, even more significantly, the "natural deviltry" of its citizens. After all, in Cuba there are many cats, dogs and cocks, which seem "as natural to Cuban soil as darkeys and fleas." This type of racial reasoning functions as a self-serving justification which reveals an underlying sense of superiority through the negative authoritative opinions of the four Americans —all Europeans in ancestry— visiting Cuba. Once again, these statements and others are symptomatic of what Orientalism meant to Said when he stated

> Orientalism expresses and represents ... [the] past culturally and even ideologically as a mode of discourse with supporting institutions, vocabulary, scholarship, imagery, doctrines, even colonial bureaucracies and colonial styles ... Orientalism is a style of thought based upon an ontological and epistemological distinction made between "the Orient" and (most of the time) "the Occident" ... [Also, Orientalism is] the corporate institution for dealing with the Orient —dealing with it by making statements about it, authorizing views of it, describing it, by teaching it, settling it, ruling it; in short, Orientalism as a Western style for dominating, restructuring, and having authority over the Orient ... European culture gained in strength and identity by setting itself off against the Orient as a sort of surrogate and even underground self.[22]

Although Cuba is not located in the Orient, we can infer that in the American imagination, inhabitants of the Caribbean country are still regarded as "other." Cuba is space undefined by geography, an example of the non-European. Upon examining the concept of Orientalism, one attempts to facilitate the study of aspects of European domination upon the foreign.[23] In this context, the European/United States referent acquires, implicitly, superiority due to the preeminence assigned to the cultural/moral standing of the citizens of the American nation. Cuba's reality as an example of otherness—of the Oriental— exists in function with the United States and the European continent, places of orgin for those leading "the land of the free and home of the brave."[24] Needless to say, we are very much aware that Cuba has never been part of the Orient. This fact lacks significance because with the term Orientalism one is referring to the European-American representation —often imperialistic— of foreign realities. Significantly, however, several times the narrator of *Souvenir* appears to be conscious of the fact that the American paradigm was far from perfect. Examples of these are afforded by a reference to the treatment received by the Chinese and voting irregularities in Denver while speaking about the torture endured by both horses and bulls during the bullfights in Havana:

> Yet in the United States practices equally as demoralizing and outrageous had often been tolerated: The assaults on the Chinese in Denver and elsewhere were far more damnable; variety exhibitions had been given in Denver much more demoralizing, and farther reaching; some of the outrages tolerated at the polls in Denver had been more disastrous to the institutions which make an American look upon the Stars and Stripes in a foreign part with a thrill of pride, than bull fighting is to any Cuban or Spanish principles of government. ("The Forts")[25]

Insofar as Cuba is concerned, *Souvenir* is not limited to Havana. There are references to other types of life within Cuba (namely, those in Guanabacoa, Regla, Marianao, Cerro, Matanzas, Yumuri Valley, Monserrat Chapel, Toledo Sugar Factory, etc.). All of them —along with numerous drawings, photographs/engravings, menus, programs, tickets and documents which accompany the narrative— shed light on aspects of the Cuban experience.

The Manuscript

It consists of four hundred and seventy-five handwritten pages, 22.5 cms. x 17.5 cms. The penmanship is clear. Throughout the manuscript there are many illustrations. Business cards, a passport, and hotel bills are also included at the end of the book (they are not reproduced). The manuscript was purchased by the University of Colorado at

Boulder Libraries from a New Yorker who inherited it from her father. The parents of this person were given, in turn, the book some time before.

Finally, the manuscript concludes with several appendices. Among them, two are very useful: a chronological listing of the four travelers' geographical advancements and a listing of their chief expenses.

Acknowledgments

I am deeply indebted to Dean James F. Williams, II, Libraries, University of Colorado at Boulder, for authorizing the reproduction of Mr. Woodbury's manuscript, to Sandy Adler for facilitating the transcription of the manuscript, and to Laura Kusnyer for suggesting changes to my introduction. To the Norlin Library and Denver Public Library staff and my secretary, Marilyn Mensing, my gratitude for their tactical support. Last but not least, my appreciation to my wife, Jeanne, for her sympathetic ear as I labored on this project and for the many constructive suggestions she made.

NOTES

1. In *Manuscript Biography of Roger Williams Woodbury*, it is indicated that he is a ninth-generation descendent of William Woodbury, who had emigrated to America from Somersetshire, England, in 1628. A substantive portion of the information available on Mr. Woodbury's life —primarily up to his arrival in Denver in 1866— comes from this unpublished *Manuscript Biography* (4 vols., housed at Norlin Library, University of Colorado at Boulder; once again, in all probability Roger authored this text as well). Other sources on his biography are Stuart Cuthbertson, "Milestones, Cornerstones, and Sidelights of the University of Colorado," *University of Colorado Bulletin* 40.17 (July 1940), William Eugene Davis, *A History of the University of Colorado, 1861-1963*, Doctor of Education Dissertation (University of Colorado, 1963), William N. Byers, *Encyclopedia of Biography of Colorado*, vol. 1 (Chicago: The Century Publishing and Engraving Company, 1901), LeRoy R. Hafen, ed., *Colorado and Its People*, vol. 2 (New York: Lewis Historical Publishing Co., Inc.), Frank Hall, *History of the State of Colorado*, vol. 3 (Chicago: The Blakely Printing Company, 1891), *History of the City of Denver, Arapahoe County, and Colorado* (Chicago: O. L. Basking & Co., 1880), Edith Eudora Kohl, *Denver's Historic Mansions. Citadels to the Empire Builders* (Denver: Sage Books, 1957), Walter Licht, *Industrializing America. The Nineteenth Century* (Baltimore: The Johns Hopkins UP, 1995), Nolie Mumey, *Nathan Addison Baker (1843-1934)* (Denver: The Old West Publishing Company, 1965), *Representative Men of Colorado in the Nineteenth Century* (Denver: The Rowell Art Publishing Company, 1902), Wallace Hayden Rex, *Colorado Newspapers. Bibliography 1859-1933* (Denver: Biographical Center for Research, Rocky Mountain Region/Denver Public Library and the State Department of Education, 1939), and Wilbur Fisk Stone, *History of Colorado*, vol. 1 (Chicago: The S.J. Clarke Publishing Company, 1918).

2. He attended high school.

3. Aspects of American economic and cultural life in the Northern states during the 1840s and 1850s are discussed by John A. Garraty, *The American Nation. A History of the United States*, 3rd ed. (New York: Harper & Row, 1975), pp. 336-67, and Samuel Eliot Morison, Henry Steele Commager and William E. Leuchtenburg, *The Growth of the American Republic*, vol. 1 (New York: Oxford UP, 1969), pp. 453-67 and 494-98.

4. Also, for a while, he was the Secretary of this organization.

5. She was a member of the Excelsior Literary Association as well.

6. One source indicates that he came with his father and mother to Colorado when he was five years old (Kohl 86). Years later, he followed his father's footsteps in business. Frank died on May 29, 1935.

7. As we shall soon see, during Roger and Anna's 1886 trip, numerous references are made to his participation in the Civil War as they traveled through the Southern states on their way to Florida.

8. He also became a compositor for the *Golden Transcript*.

9. On June 14, 1855, Mr. Koons was an advisory member of the Seventeenth General Synod of the Evangelical Lutheran Church in Dayton, Ohio. He fought in the Civil War and was married to Anna Koons, the future wife of Roger Williams Woodbury (she was a daughter of John Peterson, of Springfield, Ohio). While in Denver, Mr. Koons was also a pastor of the Lutheran Church (at the corner of Arapahoe and H Streets). In June 1867, he was listed as Editor and Proprietor of the *Daily Colorado Tribune*, whereas Mr. Woodbury was the Associate Editor of the publication (earlier the newspaper had been called the *Christian Radical*). By July 1869, Mr. Koons was no longer listed in the newspaper masthead. By then, R. W. Woodbury and John Walters figured as co-editors of the publication. Eventually, Mr. Woodbury was the only owner of the *Colorado Tribune*.

10. We are told in the *Manuscript Biography* that Anna Woodbury objected to the sale of the newspaper.

11. An announcement of their wedding was published in the *Daily Rocky Mountain News* 10. 287 (July 29, 1870). Curiously, in the 1870s Census of the United States (dated June 4, 1870), Mrs. Anna Koons (age thirty, from Ohio, a widow), resided with her two children, Mary Alice (age ten, from Illinois) and Ernest E. (age eight, from Illinois). In the 1880 U.S. Census (dated June 9, 1880), Mrs. Anna Koons became Mrs. Anna Woodbury (age forty). She resided with her husband, Roger W. (age thirty-nine), and their children Mary Alice (age twenty), Frank (age nineteen; he was her stepson) and Ernest E. (age eighteen). Although Mary Alice and Ernest E. were listed as Mr. Woodbury's daughter and son, they were his stepchildren (their last names were listed as Woodbury in the 1880 Census record).

12. For this purpose, he secured funds from Andrew Carnegie.

13. Further indication of Mr. Woodbury's prominence in Colorado is evidenced by the fact that at his funeral among his pall bearers were Senator H. M. Teller and Governor James H. Peabody. See "Pay Tribute to Late Pioneer," *The Denver Republican* (July 15 and 16, 1903).

14. In Woodbury's case, his many activities concerned life in a Western frontier city. Information on the rise of big business in the United States during the last few decades of the 19th century is provided by Louis M. Hacker, *The Triumph of American Capitalism. The Development of Forces in American History to the End of the Nineteenth Century* (New York: Columbia UP, 1947), pp. 374-424, W. Licht (pp. 133-156), John Tripple, "The Robber Baron in the Gilded Age: Entrepreneur or Iconoclast?," in *The Gilded Age. A Reappraisal*, H. Wayne Morgan, ed. (Syracuse: Syracuse UP, 1963), 14-37, and *In Their Own Words. Robber Barons and Radicals*, edited by T. J. Stiles (New York: Perigee Book, 1997, 107-48 and 315-24; it contains texts by Charles Francis Adams, Thomas N. Miller, and Andrew Carnegie).

15. In a retrospective of his life published over sixty years later, we are told that his son Frank moved into the family home upon his death ("Woodbury Contributes Greatly to Denver's Past," *Denver Times* 74.31 [1966], 1-2). Earlier, in 1903, it was indicated in his obituary that Roger was survived by this same son ("Death of R. Woodbury. One of Colorado's Greatest Citizens Called to His Final Rest," *The Denver Republican* [July 13, 1903]); the *Denver Post* also lists his wife

as a survivor (July 13, 1903). In the retrospective article of 1966, it is indicated that his wife Anna died two years after Mr. Woodbury (p. 2; something similar was stated by Darlene Wycoff, "Another Landmark of Denver is Gone," *Rocky Mountain News* [March 10, 1966] and Frances Melrose, "Woodbury Built Mansion with News Fortune," *Rocky Mountain News* [June 26, 1983]). Finally, his daughter-in-law, Mrs. Grace Lobach Woodbury, the second wife of his son Frank, explained in 1966 that Roger and Anna Woodbury were separated when Roger died and that their mansion in Denver was lost in the Panic of 1893 (see: Pasquale Marrazino, "Heartbreak and Memory," *Rocky Mountain News* [March 19, 1966]; by the time Grace Woodbury joined the family, Roger and Anna had been dead for some time). In sum, factual questions remain involving Roger and Anna Woodbury, questions which have not been resolved in local archives (Colorado records are incomplete during this period).

16. "Victorian Culture in America" *Victorian America* (Philadelphia: U of Pennsylvania P, 1979), 3-28.

17. On the subject of travel during the Victorian era, refer to Thomas J. Schlereth, *Victorian America Transformations in Everyday 1877-1915* (New York: Harper Publishers, 1991), 19, and Adam Hart-Davis, *What the Victorians Did for Us* (London: Headline Book Publishing, 2001), 90 and 176.

18. "Dios" is incorrectly used in place of "días" by Mike while Roger confuses "soy" with "estoy" in his remark "Yo estoy un mentiroso," not to mention the questionable meaning of this sentence —its fit— at the time it was pronounced.

19. As indicated, from time to time the text contains mistakes in the spelling of Spanish words (including names). Repeated mistakes contribute to the playfulness and humor which prevail throughout the book. On other occasions these errors reflect a lack of knowledge on the part of the speakers and/or the narrator. In all instances, the aforementioned "mistakes" do not obscure the book's content, as it is obvious what is being discussed. All errors have been retained being as they are an integral part of the text.

20. With its publication in book form, Woodbury's manuscript joins the growing bibliography on Cuba during the 1880s. See, among others, James W. Steele, *Cuban Sketches* (New York: G. P. Putman's Sons, 1881), Xavier Marmier, *Lettres sur l'Amérique*, vol. 2 (Paris: E. Plon et Cie; 1881), Ernest L'Epine, *Un parisien dans Les Antilles* (Paris: Librairie Plon, 1883), John Mark, *Diary of My Trip to America and Havana* (Manchester: A. Ireland & Co., Printers, 1885), James McQuade, *The Cruise of the Montauk* (New York: Thomas R. Knox & Co., 1885), F. Moreno, *Cuba y su gente* (Madrid: Establecimiento Tipográfico de Enrique Teodoro, 1887), Tesifonte Gallego García, *Cuba por fuera* (Habana: La Propaganda Literaria, 1890).

21. See Stuart B. Schwartz's views on the subject. "Introduction," *Implicit Understandings: Observing, Reporting and Reflecting on the Encounters Between Other Europeans and Other People in the Early Modern Era* (Cambridge: UP, 1994), 3-4.

22. *Orientalism* (New York: Pantheon Books, 1978), 2-3.

23. Others studying Orientalism include Tzvetan Todorov, *On Human Diversity. Nationalism, Racism, and Exoticism in French Thought*, trans. Catherine Porter (Cambridge: Cambridge UP, 1993), David Spurr, *The Rhetoric of Empire.*

Colonial Discourse in Journalism, Travel Writing and Imperial Administration (Durham: Duke UP, 1993), John M. MacKenzie, *Orientalism. History, Theory and the Arts* (Manchester: Manchester UP, 1995), and Reina Lewis, *Rethinking Orientalism: Women, Travel, and the Ottoman Harem* (New Brunswick: Rutgers UP, 2004). In Todorov's case, he avails himself of the concept of ethnocentricity as he refers to the tendency of some to consider the values of one's own culture as universal and, therefore, true (1-2).

24. Ironically, the United States had been a British colony until 1776. Nevertheless, in *Souvenir of Florida & Cuba* its citizens seem to share some of the feelings of superiority so typical among Europeans.

25. Finally, on diverse occasions negative racially motivated references are made about the nature of blacks in the United States (including those made by Roger Woodbury, a Union veteran who fought on the side of those favoring the emancipation of blacks during the Civil War).

ROGER WILLIAMS WOODBURY

SOUVENIR OF FLORIDA & CUBA 1886

PREFACE.

In the winter of 1884 three American gentlemen of Denver, with their wives, successfully disposed of several weeks on the Pacific coast, which has been described in detail in that anonymous but standard volume of travel entitled "A Souvenir of California," and which rapidly ran through an edition of three volumes. One morning nearly two years later, the three gentlemen being present within the hospitable precincts of the Union Bank, it was suggested by Roger that a trip to Cuba would neutralize the winter of 1886, and be a good joke upon importunate creditors. One of these suggestions touched Mike in a tender place, while George acknowledged the soft impeachment of the other by seizing his hat to go and ascertain the best route and the lowest price by which the Cuban shores could be reached. After a week's suspense, Mike and Roger, seeing no more of George, employed Prof. Dyer to give them instruction in the Spanish tongue on Sunday and Wednesday evenings, so that during the few weeks before departure they progressed sufficiently to be able to shake the head fluently in response to any question included in the first fifty pages of "Robertson's Español." George never appeared again until a few days before Mike's departure to spend the holidays with relatives in Ohio, and then only to express regret at an enforced absence from the city. Olive, in the meanwhile, declared the existence of a strong inclination on her part to join the party without him.

Mike departed on the 16th of December, expecting to save by his absence the expense of Christmas presents at home, but from hints that were now and then dropped subsequently it is thought that the plan did not work so well as was expected.

Roger has expected for various reasons to remain in Denver until the latter part of January, but finally overruled them all and prepared to follow Mike on the 30th of December, telegraphing him accordingly; but it being returned with the information that he could not be found on Main Street (Dayton), Roger was uncertain if they would meet at all. On the afternoon of departure he met the Directors and members of the Chamber of Commerce at their request, at the Chamber building, and which was described as follows in the "Rocky Mountain News" of the 31st:

A GRACEFUL TRIBUTE.

The Chamber of Commerce Recognizes the President's Services.

A Memorial and Resolutions With a Substantial Equivalent Behind Them.

An adjourned meeting of the Chamber of Commerce was held in the office of Secretary Hall yesterday afternoon. The meeting was called to order by James T. Cornforth, when M.J. McNamara, esq., read the following memorial and resolutions:

In recognition of the eminent services rendered this association by the president, R.W. Woodbury, and in view of his early departure from the city and state, to be absent some months on a vacation rendered necessary by the impairment of his health through constant devotion to the interests of this association, the following expression of sentiment entertained by each officer and member of the Chamber is hereby ordered to be suitably engrossed and presented by the first vice president:

Resolved, That the Denver Chamber of Commerce and Board of Trade, organized during

AN IMPORTANT CRISIS

in the history of the city, when unanimity of action by the merchants and manufacturers, under the most careful and judicious direction of the force thus created, was required to avert impending dangers, has been brought to its present stage of power and influence in a very large degree by the energy, ability and untiring zeal of its presiding officer; that we fully realize the extent and value of the aid thus afforded by one whose uniform courtesy and calm, clear judgment, under every condition, has successfully met and mastered the exigencies of every situation as it rose, thereby inspiring the entire body with profound respect and confidence in his leadership; that as chairman of the building committee

WE OWE HIM GRATEFUL APPRECIATION

for his unremitting watchfulness and care in the conduct of the work and in the expenditure of the funds; that in the superb temple of trade thus erected and the great institutions established therein, a lasting monument to the enterprise of the city is presented to the view of all strangers within our gates, whereby every artery of trade has been stimulated and strengthened, and Denver made known throughout the land as one of its great and permanently progressive cities; that in all that he has done, the fruits are shown in the improved condition of our internal affairs. Therefore, in the journey upon which he is about to enter he will be attended by a hearty "God speed" from this association, with earnest wishes for the complete restoration of his health, and by the hope that he may return in proper season to again assume the headship of newly organized forces for

A STILL MORE BRILLIANT ERA

of progress and prosperity.

Mr. McNamara then said the pleasant duty devolves upon me to present you with this slight token of our esteem and our wishes that you may have a safe journey.

Mr. McNamara then presented Mr. Woodbury with an envelope containing a check for $1,000.

Mr. Woodbury in response said:

Gentlemen and Friends: —I don't know of any position in which a man could be placed that would be so undesirable and yet so desirable as that in which I find myself. I feel myself totally inadequate to express what I feel. Of course this is not entirely a surprise. When I have seen knots of men gathered together, a meeting of the Chamber called without my knowledge, I could not but suspect that you intended to give me a pleasant good bye, but I had no conception that you intended to send me away with a full pocket. I have worked hard for two years and the gratification of knowing that these efforts

HAVE BEEN APPRECIATED

is sufficient, and I had not needed this evidence of your esteem. The opportunity I have enjoyed rarely comes to a man. To work for my fellow citizens I esteem a privilege rather than a labor. When I took the position I had grave doubts of being able to accomplish much. If what has been done is valuable my time and labor has not been thrown away. I had thought to go away when there was no important work of the chamber to be done, but I am satisfied that time will not come, and I have chosen the end of the fiscal year to go away and get that rest which I so much need."

Mr. Leight then made some remarks testifying to his long acquaintance with Mr. Woodbury and his high appreciation of his character and his great services in behalf of the chamber and the people of Denver.

After Mr. Leight's address the meeting adjourned.

Alice and her children were left at 362 13th Street, with the parents of her old schoolmate Florence Lee; and the house that was so promptly burglarized in '84 was once again locked and left to its fate. "A.J." being particularly interested in the trip, having spent two winters in Cuba, and still being able to speak several Spanish Sunday School words with native volubility, took charge of Roger's satchels to the depot by the help of James Davis; while Frank joined the voyageurs on the street cars. The Kansas Pacific train departed at 8:05 in the evening, and the sleeper was well filled, amongst the passengers being a German from Old Mexico, who inquired with a shrug and a shiver if Denver always possessed such cold winter weather. To within a few days the temperature had been too warm for comfort, but a couple of inches of snow had sent the mercury down a few degrees below freezing. The stranger had only been in Denver since morning, and on being informed by Roger that sometimes the temperature was fifty degrees colder, he looked incredulous, but very glad to escape from it so soon. And he was fortunate withal, for in a few days the railroad was blocked with snow, and remained so for over two weeks. Col. C.N. Pratt, formerly of the Greeley, Longmont, and Colorado Springs colonies, was also a passenger, and sought to interest Roger in a new scheme in "Sunny San Luis," to which Roger replied that if the Cubans let him escape with any money he might then think of it. Another passenger was H.H. Metcalf, the stockman, and conversation developed that he was formerly an officer of the Third Rhode Island Heavy Artillery, with which Roger was well acquainted, and together they spent a couple of hours in recalling men and incidents. The Pullman conductor was Charlie Stampson, of Denver, whom Roger made a Knight-Templar, and who exhibited to Roger an unabbreviated "key," alleged to be the Templar work, and which he "borrowed" from the colored porter, who informed him that it was the "Work" the colored men used in Cheyenne. He also had a manuscript work which Roger recognized as in the chirography of George M. Howe.

In the morning after breakfast at Ellis, Roger commenced a review of his Spanish, which being observed by his German acquaintance of the night before, the latter informed him that he was an excellent Spanish scholar, and he would be gratified to give him any assistance; and to illustrate his qualifications, pointed out a few words in the book which he claimed were incorrectly employed. Roger thanked him for his kindness but concluded that he had better abide by the text.

Roger and Anna relieved the buffet of half a chicken at 12:30, preferring not to await the regular station at Topeka at 3:15. There Roger renewed the acquaintance of General Nelson Miles, who like himself was wandering about the platform; and at 6 in the evening arrived at Kansas City and supped in the depot hotel, Roger first uselessly telegraphing to St. Louis for an O.&M. section to Cincinnati. Leaving Kansas City in section 7 in the Wabash sleeper, they arrived at St. Louis at 7 o'clock New Year's morning, enjoying an agreeable breakfast at the Laclede, where the head waiter remembered them well enough to call them by name. Roger again reviewed war matters with proprietor Sperry, and called at Mr. Kaime's office, but found it closed on New Year's. Roger lounged about the hotel most of the day, and discussed medicine with Ernest, who spent most of the New Year with Anna. Reporters of the "Globe-Democrat" and the "Chronicle" interviewed Roger on the business and prospects of Denver, and made particular inquiries as to Governor Tabor's financial condition, but Roger declined to answer questions of a personal nature. Being unable to obtain any positive information from the sleeper agent at the Union Depot relative to a section telegraphed for on the O. and M., Roger went to the up-town office of the company and secured section 6; and taking the train at 7 in the evening, with but few other passengers, they arrived at Cincinnati, at 7:00 in the morning, January 2^d, in the rain.

CINCINNATI TO JACKSONVILLE.

Roger having heard nothing from Mike since the latter left Denver, and the Dayton telegram having been returned undelivered, and the connection therefore being somewhat uncertain, it was with considerable gratification that the two wanderers through the long depot beheld Mike at the gate with an anxious cast of countenance, chewing upon some astounding Spanish phrase, with which he might welcome them, and at the same time assume the leading position as interpreter. "Buenos Dios," exclaimed he, with outstretched hands and a thrill of pride, to which Roger heartily responded with "Yo estoy un mentiroso." Anna experienced a glow of intense satisfaction at being associated with men who could so readily converse in a foreign tongue, while the hackmen, thinking they were nothing less than foreign Counts, and therefore unacquainted with schedule prices, rushed upon them with blended looks of hope and anxiety. But when Roger and Anna entered a fifty-cent 'bus, and Mike started away on foot, they gazed after them with unspeakable disgust. At the rather elegant Burnet House Jane was found in youthful spirits, which were at once heightened by the prospect of many weeks of confidential communications as Anna whispered in her ear that she felt certain her bonnet was not on straight. As the rain fell all day the ladies obtained a good start, while the gentlemen reviewed one lesson in Spanish, two in billiards, and three in cribbage; besides wandering in a lost kind of way up the street in the rain, which was so exceedingly wet and dismal that they dodged into a convenient ticket office that appeared inviting, and purchased Jacksonville tickets for that evening, instead of waiting several days as was at first contemplated.

Their route was by the "East Tennessee Short Line," but as all lines claim to be "short" they never imagined that it was any shorter than any other "short" line. Railroad managers delight in representing their lines as "short" from one point to another, but very long in the aggregate number of miles managed. Their train left at 8:47 p.m., and they had sections "C" and "D" in the center of the "North Star" of the Mann Boudoir line, but before leaving, Roger telegraphed home for news of the family to be wired him Sunday night to the "Carleton" at Jacksonville. None of the party had ever before traveled in a Mann car, which was partitioned into separate rooms, each opening into a passageway along one side, while their particular sections were also connected by a door between them. One side of each section was occupied by a sofa, which at night was metamorphosed into a bed, while at the same time the back of the sofa was raised on a hinge to a horizontal position, and so fastened for an upper berth, both being wide and of good length, and leaving plenty of standing room upon the floor for disrobing, as well as wall space for the hanging of clothing. The doors could be locked at the will of the occupants, who could also take their meals in their rooms from baskets or buffet, or smoke at pleasure. Their plan at meal times was to open the door between the sections, have the tables belonging to the two placed against the opening, so that each couple sitting on their sofa would thus occupy the two ends of an extension table. During smoking time the ladies occupied one room with the connecting door closed, while the caballeros Spanished and smoked and lolled in the other. Being so comfortably situated a couple of small bottles of beer were ordered at night—one for each of the ladies, but after being uncorked it was unfortunately discovered that they were not fond of it, so that Mike and Roger were obliged to drink it or see it wasted by the porter, who seemed quite anxious to begin. Poor porter.

The next day being Saturday the artist of the expedition spent the time usually allotted to sleeping in church to the production of the following graphic sketch; with the door opened between the two sections, and the tables set for use:

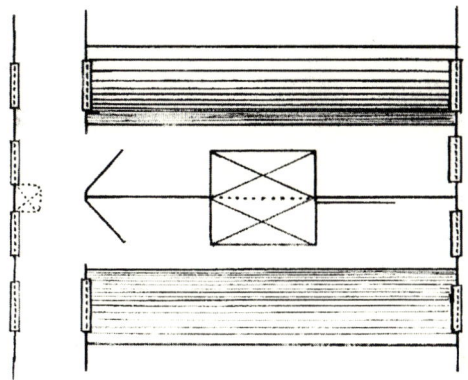

A table top and a short step-ladder were kept beneath each sofa, and the latter served the double purpose of legs for the table top and assisting ascent to the upper berth. It also had a triple use, invented on the spot by Roger, which was that of a boot-jack. Envious persons not endowed with the genius of invention, may attempt to ridicule the size of a foot from which the boot could be pulled with a step-ladder, but there is compensation in the well-established fact that almost all great inventions must first pass through a season of ridicule before their merits are fully recognized, and honors and wealth lavished upon the inventor.

Being awake at intervals during the night the rain was heard falling upon the roof in a continuous "long roll," and they were not surprised in the morning to discover the country flooded with water, I'mpetuous torrents pouring along the valleys and roadways, and seeming even to threaten the pines and oaks in their rootings in the red and yellow soil. The wagon roads were impassable, and several wide valleys, where no water ordinarily existed except perhaps little murmuring brooks, were transformed into wide and rapid rivers, sweeping along with majestic impetus, bearing away fences, and woodpiles and logs in their course, and might even have floated large steamboats.

MOCCASIN BEND AND CHATTANOOGA FROM THE POINT, LOOKOUT MOUNTAIN.

About half-past nine in the morning the train swept past a green hill-side on the left, whose well-kept sward, evenly-trimmed trees, and general appearance of taste and beauty marked it as possessing a Record or being the abode of Wealth. The graceful staff at the summit, from which floated the Stars and Stripes, told that it could justly claim both—that dead men rested there who were rich in patriotism and in the performance of duty; and who wrote with their blood the fair, the heroic, and the grand historic page which tells of Chattanooga and Lookout Mountain. Brave boys! Whom any man should be proud to call comrades! The first sight of their green graves, conspicuous from the surrounding country being bare with the desolation of winter, created an inward satisfaction that though the rain beats upon them, and the snow covers them with its cold mantle, though their bodies have long since resolved into their original elements, and their very names have passed into oblivion, yet their brave deeds are kept fresh and their memory green by the will of the people whose government they preserved. It was an honor to wear the army blue, even if soiled and ragged from the long march and dusty bivouac, but it was a greater honor to be picked up dead after stopping a rebel bullet, for how can Death come more gloriously than in support of a

Principle believed to be right? Such a death will atone in the next world for a million mistakes in this.

> "Oh, why should the spirit of mortal be proud?
> Like a swift-fleeting meteor, a fast-flying cloud,
> A flash of the lightning, a break of the wave,
> Man passeth from life to his rest in the grave.
>
> * * * *
>
> "For we are the same our fathers have been;
> We see the same sights our fathers have seen;
> We drink the same stream and view the same sun,
> And run the same course our fathers have run.
>
> * * * *
>
> "'Tis the wink of an eye, 'tis the draught of a breath,
> From the blossom of health to the paleness of Death;
> From the gilded saloon to the bier and the shroud,
> Oh, why should the spirit of mortal be proud?"

Nearly twenty-three years had swept by since Grant, Sherman, Hooker and their associates repaired Rosecrans' failure at Chickamauga by the brilliant battles of Lookout Mountain, Chattanooga and Missionary Ridge, which started Bragg on his retreat to the South, and finally let Sherman into Atlanta and down through Georgia to the Sea. When these battles occurred Mike was raiding and foraging and laying the foundation for his subsequent reputation as a rifleman, amongst the Confederates of Virginia, while Roger was taking a breathing spell in Charleston harbor, after the successful campaign on Morris Island, and the demolition of Fort Sumter.

A few minutes after passing the National Cemetery the train arrived in the suburbs of Chattanooga, with the rugged outlines of Lookout Mountain towering on its flank, and the rain-washed remains of an old earthwork occasionally visible on the elevated points. The train swept across many muddy streets and doubled back through a large part of the lower section of the city, which possessed an air of thrift and importance but not of neatness. The iron and coal that abounded noted its importance to a large area of country, and doubtless at the proper season and in favorable weather there would be beauty as well. It was too wet to venture from the depot, and the train being behind time they were soon again speeding southward. A few minutes later the train passed through the tunnel beneath Missionary Ridge, which after the battle over and along the summit was filled with the wounded and dead of both armies. Looking back from the rear of the flying train the low hills and their scrubby oaks were watched with historic interest until lost in the distance and falling rain.

All day long they found the country flooded, little gullies transformed into raging torrents, many timbers sweeping by, and the occasional old earthworks so pelted and beaten with the rain that it seemed as if they should have long ago been driven to a level with the surrounding country. At Dalton, from which Sherman flanked Johnston with his accustomed strategy, more old earthworks were observed on the hills, as dilapidated as the little town itself. Near here was observed the first cotton fields. The country was rolling and about one-half covered with woods, the settlements sparse, with but little land under cultivation. The farm houses were old and mostly of logs or "shakes"—all occupied by men who refused to repair them in the rain because it was wet; and in the sunshine because then they did not require it. Along in the afternoon they arrived at Rome, having the appearance of thrift and importance, with one large building on an eminence at the left like a State edifice. A substantial bridge spanned the Tallapoosa river at the depot, but the rain still kept the party indoors and prevented any explorations except with a young colored boy from the rear of the car.

Mike not being able to speak Spanish very well, and Roger realizing the necessity for more practice, in that tongue, inquired of the boy, "Como se llama de esta ciudad?" The young fellow cocked his head like a pullet, rolled his white eyes in a comical wondering way, and concluding that he had not exactly caught the words, replied: "What's dat you say, boss?" At which Roger failing to keep a serene countenance,

Mike took it up and repeated the inquiry in United States, which the darkey at once recognized, and after replying, laughed with great glee at Roger's mistake in having taken him for a Frenchman, and addressed him in that tongue.

South of Rome for many miles the country became almost mountainous, more broken and rugged than they supposed existed in the Southern States. Only a small fraction was settled, and it was mostly wooded with pine and oak. The rain still fell, and wherever was a route to a lower level thither the muddy streams continued to hasten.

Upon arriving at Atlanta at 3:30 in the afternoon, and observing just at the edge of town some old earthworks fronting the North, they were reminded of the sharp correspondence between Sherman and Hood, wherein the latter accused Old Tecumseh of cruelty in ordering the evacuation of Atlanta by noncombatants; and Sherman retaliated by accusing Hood of defending the city, peopled by his (Hood's) friends, so near its dwellings, that they were continually under the Northern fire. The city appeared large, hilly, and muddy—the houses on the right uniform in size, color, and "previous condition of servitude." On the left at some distance, were evidences of many large brick edifices, and all looked thrifty notwithstanding the rain and mud, and the consequent absence of people on the streets. This, then, was the city, which next to Richmond and Vicksburg, was of the most importance to the rebels to retain, and which the Union was determined to secure. To ride from the Ohio River all night and all day at a rapid rate, as straight toward Atlanta as "short lines" ordinarily run, and to conceive of leading an army all that distance from its base of supplies, with but a single line of track to connect it with reinforcements, causes an involuntary admiration of Sherman and his lieutenants; and no wonder that Hood thought after the fall of Atlanta, that by marching North and breaking this long line, which he could do in a hundred places, he could force Sherman to retreat. But he made a mistake in giving Sherman ample time to load up for another line of march, and get rid of his sick and wounded, so that when Hood started North to drag Sherman after him, the latter promptly headed to the South, leaving Hood to destruction at Franklin and Nashville.

The train arrived at Macon about 7 in the evening, where it was raining a little, and too dark to see the city. There was a high bank above the depot platform, reached by a long flight of stairs, with a street-car line nearby. Roger sought to induce Mike to make a speech from the top of the stairs, while the former comprised the large and enthusiastic audience from the platform below, but Mike refused without the usual stipend to lecturers, expenses paid, which Roger would not guarantee, and therefore the project failed.

In the evening the gentlemen enjoyed a long conversation with Mr. C.H. Foster of Boston, going to his winter residence at Manatee, who invited them to call and see him at the latter place. If they desired a country home in Florida, he recommended them to write to John G. Webb of Osprey, Manatee Co., near where they would find good alligator hunting. He said that 18 miles East of Webb's, was a small lake, to which a party of 5 or 6 ladies and gentlemen went hunting, and in less than a week killed over 700 'gators, which were so numerous in the lake that when sunning themselves a man might walk across the lake upon their backs. Mr. Foster said there was nothing so gratifying to the palate of a fastidious 'gator as a young pig or a "nigger" baby, and the hunting party aforesaid engaged in the slaughter for the protection of the former.

The last night of this most agreeable journey by rail was too warm for comfort. Anna declared in the morning that she spent the night in climbing the cool partition feet foremost to ally the fever in her lower extremities, but refused all solicitations for a diagram of her ascent for the journal.

When the bus-man went through the car he made out one ticket to include the whole party, which Roger thought it was wise to take possession of; then he claimed that Mike should pay him for one-half or receive no benefit from it. Mike insisted that he had paid his share to the 'bus-man and that the ticket was as much his as Roger's but the latter replied that as he has possession of the ticket it was prima-facie evidence that he had paid for it; but Mike kicked so strenuously that he waived the matter and awaited a more favorable opportunity for making expenses.

JACKSONVILLE.

The rain that had kept company with the party from Cincinnati had just begun in Florida, but on their arrival at Jacksonville at 8:30 on Monday morning they found the black flag flying, and a cold wave following close in their rear. Taking the "Carleton" bus under the management of "Thoroughbred" they were soon at the hotel, where a telegram from Alice that all were well at home caused Anna to relish her breakfast and forget all about climbing the partition during the night. After breakfast Mike and Roger sallied out to look at the city, and called upon Past

Grand Master McLean and Grand Secretary D.C. Dawkins of the Masonic Grand Lodge, the latter recognizing Roger and the former failing to do so, but both appearing glad to see him. Bay street had improved but little during the seven years since Roger was there before, but the hotel and residence portions had grown very much—showing the improvement to be by Northern people seeking winter homes, and not opportunities for business. The old Moody place where Anna and Roger had rooms in '79 had been torn down and an elegant brick mansion was being erected on its site. The gentlemen attended lodge with McLean in the morning. The quarters were quite untidy, and presented no improvement in seven years. Just before opening the master requested them to examine a visitor from Leadville named R.W. Crampton. The first sight impressed them with the belief that the "C" in his name had originally been a "T." He said that he was a member of Ionic lodge, and he had no doubt been in Leadville at one time or another, but when they began to look up the last Colorado proceedings to ascertain if his name was in the list, he promptly said that it would not be found there, because he did not send in his dimit and make application for membership until November, apparently fixing as late a date as he dared and not excite suspicion. Inquiry was made as to where he had been since leaving Leadville, and learning that he was quite a traveler they remarked upon the brief period since November, whereupon he said that he left Leadville in May but had mailed his dimit and petition for membership in November, and supposed he had been elected. The fellow was evidently ignorant of the Grand Lodge laws of Colorado, and that he had been entrapped into showing that he could not possibly hold membership in Leadville; and as Roger and Mike were asked to examine him because of his Colorado membership, they retired and informed the Master that they declined to pursue it further on that basis, but would continue on general principles if he desired. The Master not wishing to cultivate the stranger further, he was permitted to retire, and never knew what hurt him. The next morning Mike's and Roger's names appeared in the paper as being at the Carleton from Denver, and within an hour after breakfast the tramp sent up his card as from Fairplay, to

Mr. Spangler, who being at Roger's room learning to play crib, the card was taken there. Supposing the card to be for himself Roger started down accompanied by Mike, expecting to meet some millionaire miner who was spending a few Colorado thousands in Florida, and desired to squander a portion upon two such distinguished citizens of Denver. Having forgotten for the moment the name of the lodge tramp of the night before, they were considerably "taken back" when the dirty-looking fellow rose and advanced to meet them as they reached the bottom of the stairs. Evidently he had no thought in his mind of the gentlemen who "examined" him the previous evening, but supposed he had fallen upon fresh meat. Roger evinced no token of recognition as he approached, but stiffened up to receive him in as frigid a manner as possible, when the tramp opened for Roger an escape valve by inquiring if he was Mr. Spangler. Roger saw the opportunity, promptly informed him that he was not, waved his hand to Mike who was close in the rear, with the information that that was Col. Spangler, and instantly retreated up stairs. Mike followed on pretty nearly a run, having waited only long enough to hear the fellow say that he had failed to receive a "remittance," and was desirous of making a loan of fifty cents. But to return to the Lodge: It was attended by only eight or ten persons, about one-half of whom were visitors. McLean acted as Senior Deacon, and after the opening, rose and introduced the visitors to the Master and lodge officially, one by one, by name, titles, etc. The Master was new, and the Secretary old and countryfied, so that every little question that arose was followed by a tedious and uninteresting debate as if the salvation of the Lodge depended upon it. The proceedings showed that the Master had allowed a resolution appointing a committee with power to call a special meeting of the lodge, and other irregularities subversive of discipline, and illustrating the absence of a competent head for Jacksonville masonry, one competent to lead in the right road, and draw the craft after him. It was the first meeting after installation and work on the third degree was to be performed, but although the new master was unable to perform the work, the old master was not there to give his assistance in so difficult a task. Evidently he has cared only for the honor of having once been Master, and retaining the title. There is an opportunity there for strong work, so as to imbue the brethren with a loftier spirit than a desire for official honors alone.

January 11th. Mike and Roger begin a series of interesting games at Cribbage, of one thousand points each game, and the first of which was won by Mike, who scored his thousand points to Roger's 976. This important feature of the two and a half months in which the party was together, will not be carried along day by day, but will be presented in detail at the close of the story, where future generations can study it in detail and in continuity, together with the grand total of fifty-eight games and the averages.

The party remained in Jacksonville until Thursday afternoon, January 7, during which time the gentlemen strolled over to the Cemetery near by, remarkable only for white sand and mildewed stones; called on the Honorable Mr. Higgins, collector of Customs, and found him, or his business representative, at least, to be an inferior looking colored man, but apparently a gentleman and well informed generally; exchanged greenbacks for about fifty dollars in silver, each, followed by Mike spending an hour or two in seeking to recover his greenbacks from merchants who seemed to distrust it because of the uncertainty of Congressional action, and the unsupported charges of depreciated value; played three games of billiards of 50 points each, in which Mike gave Roger fifteen points, so that the latter succeeded in scratching through; wandered along the docks and saw nothing of particular interest except some negro boys fishing through a hole in the planks, and one of them securing a catfish with a mouth as large as the hole; saw J.E. Tucker, a railroad land commissioner, formerly of Denver, and who preferred to live in the latter; went out riding with the ladies, taking in Brooklyn and past the residence of Gen. F.E. Spinner of chirographic fame; Roger was weighed on the 6th, and was found to have increased from 143 to 145 pounds, since leaving Denver.

Here in Jacksonville the first alligators of the season were seen, there being many small ones for sale to tourists, but Mike and Roger having planned a grand hunt later on, they invested nothing on this occasion. On the street one day while Mike was

 seeking to change his silver back into greenbacks, they saw a drunken fellow on horseback, whom a policeman was endeavoring to arrest, that created much amusement. The man was drunk enough to be continually reeling in his saddle to the verge of falling, but sober enough to understand the policeman, who kept edging up like a cat to a mouse, but when just ready to seize him, the fellow would start his horse away on the jump, he reeling in all directions, while the crowd laughed as they generally do at the mishaps of a man trying to perform his duty. It is a good officer, who under such provocation from man and crowd, can keep his temper, and not attempt to "get even" with the culprit when in his possession.

One day Mike and Roger strolled over in the direction in which the latter was camped with his regiment, twenty-two years before, and when he was a young man of twenty-three, and Roger related to Mike an incident of the camp. His regiment was temporarily mounted, and had been sent down from Morris Island as a reinforcement to Gen. Trueman Seymour after his disastrous defeat at Oluster, and for incompetence in the management of which he should have been cashiered. The 3^d New Hampshire was camped just outside the town, and having lately received a lot of recruits consisting of New York "bounty-jumpers," it lost one by desertion every night or two, much to the chagrin of the old members of the Regiment. Thereupon Col. Plimpton one night quietly posted an advance picket outside of what had before been the outer post, with orders to arrest any one from either direction. About two o'clock in the morning a man approached from the direction of the regular picket post, and upon being halted, and supposing he had reached a rebel post, he announced himself as a deserter from the 3^d New Hampshire. Upon being required to dismount and give himself up, he was astonished to find himself in the hands of men of his own regiment. The next morning he was taken into camp, the Colonel organized a drums head court martial, tried him, adjudged him guilty, and shot him in an hour; and he was the last deserter from that camp.

The weather at Jacksonville during their stay was too cold for comfort, and an overcoat was usually required. The ladies enjoyed a fine opportunity to talk secrets, and Mike declared that he had a good one himself, but would not divulge it until the "history" was in press. It was supposed that he referred to the manner in which he had been treating Jane, naturally not wishing it published. A "mind-cure" doctress in Chicago, whom Jane consulted after leaving Denver, had said that she had not been treated well, and her feelings having been hurt, it had settled in her joints, but now they would be all right again. Thus will men's evil doings be brought to light when they least expect it. If this is not the secret to which Mike referred it is probable that he has long since forgotten it himself.

At the Carleton House they were introduced to Mr. Julius Rendon, connected with the Hotel San Carlos at Havana, and who concluded to take the same steamer home, with them. They had intended to sail on the new steamer Mascotte, just about to make her first trip, but as the new City of Nassau, intended to ply between St. Augustine and Nassau, had just been lost on her trial trip, and as the wind was high and another bad spell of weather predicted by the signal service, they concluded to proceed to Tampa and take the New Orleans steamer Whitney on Saturday. So purchasing tickets to this would-be-great-gulf city, they arranged to take the steamer "H.B. Plant" up the St. John's river. The "Plant" was to leave the dock at 3:30 in the afternoon, and Mike started down at 2, with the tickets, to see that the boat was ready and the purser in good spirits, as their staterooms had not been assigned. The remainder of the party and the baggage went down a half hour later. After seeing the ladies seated in the cabin Roger went around searching for Mike, but without success. After a half hour or more, he observed the "Queen of the St. John's" loaded with passengers at a dock two or three blocks away, and thinking that perhaps Mike might have been led astray to the largest boat, he hurried thither. Upon nearing the St. John's he met Mike hastening away, who having paid little attention to the name of the boat on which passage had been secured, had been awaiting their arrival at the wrong one; and becoming alarmed at their non-appearance, and seeing the "Plant" two blocks down stream, had induced the Captain of the St. John's to hold the steamer until he could go down and bring the party to the right boat. He naturally thought that he had at least a ten-dollar joke on Roger, but on learning the truth he begged hard that the Record should make no mention of the facts, but History is, or should be, the exact truth, uncolored and uninfluenced by personal objections or ambitions. It appeared that Mike had surrendered the four tickets to the Purser of the St. John's, and as they cost forty-four dollars for the party, the joke bade fair to be an expensive one for him; but he returned on board and begged or bought them back, and told the Captain not to wait any longer for the party. No one ever heard him say how much the Captain charged him for the delay, but it is well known to the entire party that before they got their staterooms on the "Plant" he expressed regret that he had not remained on the "St. John's." The tickets were finally handed to the Purser on the dock of the "Plant," who caused the trunks to be checked and wheeled on board, but he would give no satisfaction about staterooms, and did not open his office for assignment until the steamer had departed from the dock. It was delayed for an hour and a half, and did not get away until five. Mike and Roger wandered around the dock and the boat, and wondered why people ever traveled for pleasure. Mike stuck his umbrella through an orange peel that lay on the dock, and made two or three efforts to sling it into the river. At the last attempt he succeeded, and nearly lost his umbrella into the bargain, for it broke at the handle, leaving the latter in his grasp, while the major portion flew against a hawser post and lodged at the very edge of the water. He explained to the ladies that he had a dispute with a man, and being obliged to tap him on the head with his umbrella, he had in the excitement of the moment struck a little harder than was intended, and thereby broke the handle of his weapon.

JACKSONVILLE TO TAMPA

The "Plant" was crowded, and there was much uncertainty as to whom should obtain staterooms. On the dock Roger had sought to bribe the Purser with a couple of bright silver dollars, but probably the number was insufficient or he was opposed to silver, for he refused to take them. Mike thereupon posted himself at the Purser's window and waited an hour and a half for its opening. Fortified by the statement of the agent from whom they were purchased, that the tickets included staterooms, he refused to surrender them until the keys of their staterooms were placed in his hands. Roger and he had agreed that in case of "no staterooms" they should claim the assurance of the ticket seller, and demand to be placed back on the Jacksonville dock, even if the steamer had proceeded ten miles up the river. And the demand would have been made. On the "Plant" was J.F. Welborn, formerly of Denver, then residing at Winter Park, and who voluntarily sought the Captain and Purser in their behalf. The supper tables were small, and as they were in the rear at that first grand rush, they obtained but little at the second. The darkness had come before leaving the dock, the cold wave was freshening outside, and the cabin was full, so that they felt imprisoned until Mike produced the crib board, upon which the gentlemen played until beds were made all around them on the cabin floor for those who had no staterooms, Rendon amongst the rest. Roger declared that such "first-class" passage up the St. John's was even less satisfactory and comfortable than his first one, 22 years before, when he rode horseback through the swamps, ate hardtack, and slept on the ground. On that occasion his company and two others of the 3^d New Hampshire, being ferried across the river at Jacksonville, marched 75 miles to Palatka, consuming three days. Much of the way was through water, and the road indistinguishable except to the "cracker" guide. No young white men were found in the country, but on the inhabitable knolls above the swamps, a few old men and women were eking out existence on rye coffee and hoe cake. The "Maple Leaf" ferried them across the river to Palatka, where they encamped in an orange grove; made a ten-mile reconnaissance into the country the next day, fired a few shot, found no enemy, returned, found orders to evacuate, again crossed the river on the "Maple Leaf," and started down the river. At Palatka, garrisoned by Col. Jim Montgomery's negro regiment, they learned that the "Maple Leaf" had been destroyed by a torpedo the same night they left her. The rebs had set a price on Montgomery's head, they having hated him from the border-ruffian days in Kansas. Roger and the officers of the 3^d partook of his frugal meal, and found him a hawkeyed man of middle-age, tall but slightly stooping, wiry and alert. As before remarked, Roger thought that trip a more comfortable one than this.

The next morning at daybreak they were near the place called Astor, and the river and shores presented a weird and singular scene. The former had narrowed to 200 feet; its shores at long intervals rose to an elevation of six or eight feet, such oases being devoted to the cultivation of the orange; but generally there were no shores except a miscellaneous commingling of water and grasses and tall reeds stretching far away. Here and there were long-legged and long-necked white birds standing like ghostly sentinels in the rushy margin, and feeding amongst plants like immense calla lilies. At intervals the higher banks were drooping with trees and vines whose foliage had been frosted into brilliant shades of red and yellow like Northern maples; and yet again they were fringed with thin lines of palmetto and cypress, the leafless limbs of the latter reaching over the water, covered with pendant-Spanish moss, which illuminated before daybreak by the electric light from the bow of the boat, suggested that all Nature was robed in mourning garments and flowing tresses, and had wept until the land was flooded with her tears.

The "St. John's" had started three hours in advance of the smaller "Plant," but could not make the short turns in the river so readily as the latter, which frequently ran within ten feet of the shores; hence the "Plant" had overtaken the "St. John's" by daylight, but owing to the narrowness of the stream, and the maneuvers of the latter by steering across its bows, it could not pass until they reached a wide stretch known as Lake Monroe, and upon the shores of which Sanford was located. The passengers of the "Plant" were very indignant at the repeated obstructions of the "St. John's," but they had no remedy. At Sanford the Denver party were glad that they had taken passage on the "Plant," which landed at the railroad wharf, while the "St. John's" was obliged to go a quarter of a mile further, and as the rain was falling fast, and the "Plant" passengers secured all the best seats in the cars, it was quite an object. Here, however, they made another long black mark against the Purser when they discovered that he had only checked their trunks to Sanford, which necessitated their standing some time in the rain to recheck; after which they secured comfortable seats in the parlor car at fifty cents each. They had hardly started when Roger exposed his condition of fullness, for in attempting to sit down in the large arm chairs he fell with his shoulder against the large plate glass window, and broke it into fragments. He sought to make it appear to have been caused by the sudden lurching of the car, due to his stepping off from its center, but the explanation was not received with any evidence of enthusiasm. The ride to Tampa was tedious and uninteresting—the train being narrow gauge, the country very flat, and covered with pine trees, innumerable little lakes, and white sand. The town of Winter Park, the residence of Mr. Welborn, was scattered in the usual white sand and tall pines, but with an immense new hotel called the "Seminole," claimed to be the largest in the State. The party partook of the alleged dinner at Kissimmee but had nothing first-class except the sweet potatoes and price. The rain fell all day, and frequently beat in through the window casings, and at one sandy stretch when they awaited a freight train, it fell in perfect torrents.

TAMPA.

The train arrived at Tampa at five o'clock in the afternoon, which though three hours behind, was in reality a little ahead of regular time. The wind was blowing a gale, and was cold withal, so they hastened into a couple of good-looking two-horse carriages, and after a little circusing by the horses attached to that occupied by the ladies, they were driven to the St. James, which Mr. Rendon said was the best in the place. In the next twenty-four hours they sized it up to be a wonderful hotel—a uno caballo fonda y posada—a great many sizes too large for either proprietor or cook.

The parlor contained an immense fireplace with crochet work twenty inches deep fringing the opening, but the fire never succeeded in singeing it. The "St. James" illustrated the Southern style of building for warm weather alone, windows opening to the floor, with a hundred wide cracks for the cold to enter and neutralize the tender heat of the fire. The ladies wore their heaviest wraps and formed a half-circle about the fireplace, but when their teeth began to chatter and their joints to rattle the gentlemen built fires in their rooms, which contained stoves about the size of hand satchels, and which would take in 7-inch sticks of wood without chopping. After a 6 1/2-o'clock supper, so-called, and which escaped severe criticism because of hunger, the party whisted around the stove in Anna's room, and then the gentlemen adjourned to the smoky office to watch an old fellow resembling Bartow of the Leadville "Democrat," play cribbage. They inferred that he was at least a general or a judge from the air of superiority and decision with which he moved his pegs and looked at Mike and Roger to bask in their glances of approval and admiration.

The wind blew hard and cold all night, and in the morning the sky was leaden and cheerless. The gentlemen's fall overcoats were too thin, and the old cow, over which they tumbled in the yard the night before, was curled into a heap, hugging itself to keep warm. Rendon, who had no sleep the preceding night on the boat, was indignant at being called before daylight. They rattled away at his door and cried out that it was five o'clock. "Well, what's the matter with five o'clock?" said he. "The train goes in half an hour," was the reply. "Well, all right; let it go; don't hold it for me"; and he buried his head beneath the bedding, and stuffed a pillow into each ear to save myself from being roused again at 5:15. The men wrestled with the north wind to the dock, ascertained that the steamer had not arrived, and then played pool (Mike and Rendon) at a billiard saloon, in the center of which was a charcoal brazier for a stove, while the windows were all opened to expel the fumes. Having failed in obtaining much warmth there they sought it at the dinner table, which consisted of a plate and ten side dishes, each containing slush in various forms. Then they went out prospecting, and engaged rooms at the "Palmetto," to which they removed after paying the "St. James" six dollars for each couple. The new hotel was good in comparison with the latter, but had some of the same objections as to cold. But the proprietor did his best, and the society was better, and during their stay they prospered as well as could be expected under the circumstances. Saturday morning ice was found an eighth of an inch think in the hotel, and the mercury stood at 26 degrees. That day the five stoves consumed a cord of oak wood, and the owner was kept busy firing up almost the entire time. He did that part of his work well, and if he did not warm a very big spot at a time he did the best he could. Monday morning the ice was a quarter of an inch thick, and the mercury hovered around 28° until afternoon. A few flakes of snow fell, and with the leaden sky and white sandy streets, it looked as if the ground was entirely covered. That night landlord Franz coming up from the street purloined an armful of bricks from a new building, and after roasting them on the stoves, furnished them to the invalid guests for bedfellows. Tuesday morning, after an uncomfortable night for Roger of asthma, sneezing, rheumatism and frost, the mercury had crawled down to 18°, ice in the bottom of buckets was two inches thick, and water pipes were frozen. During all of this cold spell most of the guests spent the day in hugging the red-hot stoves—one side blistering and the other frosting. Many jokes were indulged in, such as that the "Mascotte" had finally forced her way through the ice in the bay, and should she be frozen in, Congress would make an appropriation for a relief vessel. As a means of taking advantage of circumstances it was proposed to inaugurate the business of storing ice for shipment to Northern cities. The weather formed the staple subject of conversation, nearly all of the twenty or more guests being there to escape the rigors of northern winters, and all agreeing that they never suffered so much at home. But when the papers arrived, and gave full accounts of the blizzard over the whole country, including freezing the tails from two monkeys in a menagerie in Georgia, greater satisfaction prevailed. The entire town during this cold spell was wrapped in gloom. Outside business was entirely suspended, except that little fires were built in the sandy streets, around which huddled crowds of blacks, who had no methods for getting warm at home. The turkey buzzards, of which there were large numbers, and which were the official scavengers, and were legally free from molestation, kept continually on the wing, as if to keep up a circulation. Ladies in private houses covered their box plants with mosquito netting as a protection from the frost. The leaves of the orange trees stiffened and turned up their bellies, while the fruit on the trees was frozen solid. A small proportion only having been picked the loss was large, even at the retail price of ten cents per dozen, which Roger paid. The trees are long-lived and very prolific, one being told of by Mr. Franz which produced a crop selling for $127.00 at one cent per orange. During this cold spell the guests were driven from the other hotels and the Palmetto became quite lively, amongst them the "Johnsons" predominating. The owner was a Johnson, and his son kept the books; a third was a son of a former United States and Confederate Senator from Missouri, who elicited the remark from Mike that he had never found out what he was born for; a fourth and fifth was his wife and child; a sixth was a dwarf who could have taken the part of one of Hendrick Hudson's goblin crew in "Rip Van Winkle" without "making up." Three other characters at the "Palmetto" may be mentioned to assist memory in the future: A chamber-maid and her daughter, the former an octoroon or a quadroon, and the latter white; the mother having been a slave, and the father of the girl the mother's master; and the colored waiter who went to the head of the stairs, the front door, and the public hall and howled when breakfast, dinner or supper was ready.

In appearance Tampa was similar to all the other Florida towns, a white sandy level with wooden buildings. The latter were scattered over a large area, as if each owner intended to be on a corner. The city seemed to be improving and two brick buildings, of fair proportions, were going up, the brick having been imported from Georgia. It was quite well sidewalked with plants. There were but few flowers to be seen and they looked as sickly as the oranges on the trees. Mike and Roger thought they would like 160 acres near the town, and selected a grove of live oaks adjacent to the mouth of Hillsborough river, from the limbs of which the Spanish moss hung down six or eight feet. When standing beneath these giant limbs they seemed to be thousands of syren arms, waving and beckoning the visitor to an embrace that, ceasing only in Death, should be transformed into an endless sadly swinging requiem over his grave.

This picturesque spot was a military reservation, and the gentlemen concluded that the site for a city must be a number of miles down the bay nearer deep water, notwithstanding the fact that all investments were at or near the existing town. Five

miles inland were being erected some thirty or more large wooden buildings by a Key West cigar firm, who had purchased 200 acres, and were alleged to be spending $2,000,000. Doubtless they will soon be heard from in the cigar markets of the country.

THE GULF OF MEXICO.

During the cold spell at Tampa the "Whitney" arrived from New Orleans and departed, but the tourists declined to take passage, preferring to await settled weather and the "Mascotte." By this delay the ladies were enabled to attend a Baptist church and make a large number of good resolutions for the future. Wednesday, January 13th, was the day for the sailing of the Mascotte, by which time the cold wave had passed, and the weather was becoming warm. After a climb by Roger and Anna to the Palmetto tower for a general view of the city and Tampa bay, the party left for the transfer steamer "Margaret," together with several other Palmetto guests, the shallow water in the bay causing the gulf steamers to anchor about five miles away from the city. Boarding the "Margaret" at 2:30 they then had to await the arrival of the Jacksonville train with the mail, during which hour they were weighed at the warehouse on the dock, with the following result: Jane 117; Anna 133; Roger, 143 1/4; Mike 410. The ladies also amazed themselves by taking coculons, and watching to see the passengers get thumped by the cabin door on the Margaret flying back into their faces when they attempted to open it. Roger sought to relieve the tedium by giving them some orange, and they laughed when he attempted to fling the peel out of the window, and it struck glass.

The train brought in a number of Havana passengers, including John Cook, Jr., of Denver, and whom Roger had prophesied some days before would be a fellow-passenger. Representatives of the Telegrafo, Inglaterra and Pasaje hotels of Havana, all having been skirting around Florida for guests, were also on board, and all of whom Rendon regretted to see for fear they would entice the Denver party to another hotel than the "San Carlos." Mike and Roger, however, were delighted to see them, and concluded to encourage them all they could without designing ingratitude to Rendon, who had really been of considerable service, and whom they had used very much as a servant. He had stuck to them like a poor relative from the time they made his acquaintance at Jacksonville, and it was a sorry prospect to him to see his particular "game" competed for by three others just when he had it almost secured. On the ride down the harbor to the "Mascotte" they passed the bones of an old sunken steamer, and from which a schooner was taking the old iron. The vessel looked as if it had been there since the war, and therefore it was concluded that it must have been a blockade runner, so as to add historical interest to the trip.

The "Mascotte" was a brand new vessel, with everything neat and clean, even to the uniforms of the officers, but its arrangements for the assignment of staterooms appeared to be on a par with those of the "Plant," for an hour passed before keys were obtained; and the Denver party was among the first to be supplied. Mike had No. 3, and Roger No. 5, on deck, in preference to staterooms rather more elaborate in the cabin. The boat was illuminated by incandescent lights, and was finished in handsome woods. After a very good supper the party whisted in the cabin, and then repaired to the deck to enjoy their first ride upon the green waters of the Gulf of Mexico. Long they sat and watched the twinkling stars and the phosphorescent waves, and speculating on the balmy climate and tropical scenes to be realized in a few hours more. The party did pretty well through the night and were all able to partake of a nice breakfast in the morning, but many of the passengers were ill. The sea was rather quiet, and neither nux nor coculons were in much demand. The morning ride to Key West was particularly agreeable, it being the first morning since the tour began that the atmosphere was not raw and chilly. Numerous islands were sighted in the distance, with now and then a remote sail looming up like a lighthouse, and about 10:15 the masts and trees and buildings of Key West slowly appeared above the horizon. The "Mascotte" sailed near to a number of outlying islands, or keys, one of which presented the regular oval appearance of a hat-crown ⬯, the trees or brush giving a symmetrical outline, and seemingly closely interwoven. Subsequently the party was informed that there was no land there within three feet of the surface of the water; but little by little mud would be gathered until finally it would rise above the water, and in time become fitted for human habitation. This particular embryonic island appeared to be several miles in circumference. Between the numerous low keys appeared a good many fishing vessels—little smacks, some at anchor, and some making port. The "Mascotte" took the shorter way in, zigzagging from buoy to buoy, with slowed engines, and the lead constantly going, showing at places only nine or ten feet of water. Amongst the outer buoys was one with a bell, so that every time the buoy rose or fell with a wave its bell sent an alarm across the waters that danger was there, and that the mariner in the dark night or the fog should take due warning. During the morning the interpreters for the Havana hotels presented their cards, some of them two or three times, and expressed almost tearful regret that they could not have the pleasure of caring for the Denver party. Roger found that he had a letter of introduction to the "Telegrafo" interpreter, one E.A. Smyrk, and consequently the latter was more disappointed than any of the others, feeling the possession of a prior right, and that Rendon had been guilty of absolute theft. Smyrk declared that they could never endure the San Carlos, and shrugged his shoulders in expressive pantomime and pity that they were resolved to be imposed upon even for a single day—at the end of which time he was positive they would repair their mistake by seeking the "Telegrafo."

As the Mascotte neared the harbor, and the city grew more and more prominent, the picture became very attractive: Old Fort Taylor and its black muzzled guns on the right, and the tapering masts of the shipping on the left, from which idly floated the graceful flag they were about to exchange for the emblem of blood and gold; the green foliage of the stately and novel cocoanut trees, interspersed between the quaint old chimneyless buildings, adding color and variety; whites and blacks thronging the wharf, clad in thin light-colored garments and straw hats—all combined to produce an impression upon the mind that should be permanent as well as pleasing. The "Mascotte" steamed slowly to the wharf, but with so much headway that before the reversal of its engines its bow cut into the rail of the "Alamo" steamship of New York, smashing the rail and a hawsehole, and badly bending the iron plating.

On the wharf were many people of different shades of white and black, mostly loafers, and amongst them a white dwarf of 28 years, two and a half feet in height, whose strut and general appearance of importance would excuse any precocious child from asking if he was God. Mike and Roger went at once on shore and sought the office of James W. Locke, Judge of the United States Court, who was an old schoolmate of Roger's. Being sent for by his brother, he soon entered, and was greeted by Roger with "How are you, Jim?" The judge shook hands and appeared rather nonplussed, so that after a few seconds Roger remarked that probably he did not remember him, but the judge said: "I believe I do after all. You remind me of Roger Woodbury," and then shook hands heartily. They had not met for twenty-four years, when Roger was camped on Hilton Head, South Carolina, and James was attached to the sloop of war "Dale," and visited the camp one day with a party of naval officers. He had aged considerably in appearance, wore a long beard, well streaked with gray, and presented something of the appearance of a Methodist clergyman on a small salary and large family—having at first sight lost the sprightly activity of his younger days. He was very slightly bent, wore a plug hat, and after a few minutes, was natural—the same good and pleasant fellow as of old. He accompanied them to the steamer, and then with the ladies all entered a one-horse two-seated carriage, with Mike perched beside the driver, and rode all over the island, which was both small and low, its highest elevation being but 15 feet. During long storms, with high winds, the water from the ocean sometimes sweeps across the island and through the streets of the city, which consists of 15,000 people, one half of whom are Cubans. At Key West they began to get touches of Cuban life, in dirty domiciles jumbled together in wondrous shapelessness, signs in Spanish, swarthy complexions, and the odor of garlic. Here they were reminded

 that they had reached a land of tropical productions, for oranges, bananas, sugar cane, etc., was everywhere for sale, and young Cubans and Darkeys regaling themselves in every direction. The "schoolmaster" was also abroad, as they read in front of a news-stand the following sign in large letters: "Open only on week days. Customers can have their papers on Sunday by calling on Saturday."

Almost everything in the nature of trees was new—one of the most interesting being the cocoanut, with its limbless trunk and shaggy top, and large bunches of green nuts of various sizes like a bunch of grapes. Another rare tree, and probably the only one in the United States, unless in some botanical garden, was a banyan, from the limbs of which shoots grew downwards, bearing at the extremity a bunch of fibers that took root upon reaching the ground. Though called a young tree its trunk and sub-trunks were twelve or fifteen feet through from side to side, while the branches shaded a very large area. The main trunk

was closely entwined with shoots that had put-down from the low limbs near it. This tree might be made a great attraction if trained by cutting away some of the down-growing roots so as to make it more symmetrical, and prevent them from interfering with passage. The southern point of Florida can sometimes be reached by rail, and possibly Key West also, as the water from key to key is shallow; and the authorities of Key West would do well to at once start a banyan forest, that would soon become a wonderful resort after the place could be thus readily reached.

A short distance from the tree was the military cemetery, in one corner of which, beneath an oblong solid tomb of concrete and brick, lay another old schoolmate of Roger, George K. Dakin. He was handsome, genial and talented, and the pride of the boys and girls who were free from envy; but like many whose youth is brilliant with sunlight, his very popularity pushed him headlong into dissipation and a drunkard's grave.

Here at Key West was also seen the acacia, that later became very familiar in Cuba, —low and wide-branched, bearing numerous very long pods, samples of which the gentlemen secured for home with the assistance of Judge Locke, which were twenty inches in length. The tree was technically known as the "Royal Poinciana." At Judge Lock's residence, where they met his wife and daughter, he also showed them the New Zealand flax lily, and partly supporting the sharp point, drew with it from the leaf a long silken thread, representing a needle and thread ready for sewing, as employed by the uncivilized people of some of the Pacific islands. Also from another leaf a 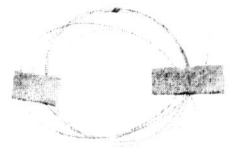 coarser thread (not here represented) known as the Sisal hemp. Beneath one of the wharves in the back part of the town, were pens containing green turtles ready for capture and shipment when required, and looking in, a dozen or twenty were seen swimming about, three or four feet across their backs, and fins stretching out fifteen inches on each side. Numerous piles of sponges around the boatmen's wharf denoted one of the chief industries of the people amongst the neighboring islands.

Visiting the market, Mike and Roger invested in two yards of sugar cane at five cents, and four great bananas at ten cents, of a negro woman who was the sole remnant of the market at that hour of the day. Sitting upon the edge of a sidewalk they

 imitated some of the natives of less years and darker hue, and then boarded the "Mascotte" for dinner. This was served with elegance, and consisted of rice soup; fish flanked with pyramids of mashed potato; browned oyster patties; beef with mushrooms and canned tomatoes; Irish and sweet potatoes, sliced turkey; apple and cranberry pie; apples; nuts; raisins; cheese; cake; ice-cream; oranges; figs; coffee and tea.

Shortly before sailing Judge Locke called with his pretty daughter "Carrie" with an immense bouquet of roses for the ladies, which before night had partially passed into the hands of the gay old Purser, for precautionary reasons relative to the return of the party on the same boat. As twilight approached the "Mascotte" prepared to depart, and as it slowly drifted away from the wharf the majestic "Brooklyn," of the United States Navy, came up on its bow. Roger did not know, as he peered through the gathering gloom, that he was probably looking straight into the face of a friend, but such afterwards appeared to be the fact, as Assistant Engineer W.F.C. Hasson, formerly of the University faculty at Boulder, was amongst its officers. Thus may the paths of friends converge from distant points after months or years, and without the knowledge of either. The "Mascotte" departed as the lights were beginning to show at the fore of the vessels at anchor, and a few miles away to the south the "Sand Key" light was already aglow on the Southernmost point of land owned by the United States. After leaving Key West and entering the Gulf Stream, proceeding only at half speed so as to make the ninety miles to Havana at sunrise, the steamer began to roll so much that most of the passengers were driven to their berths at an early hour. Nearly all the passengers were more or less seasick. Anna and Jane groaned in two or three languages. Roger descended from the top berth in which it was almost impossible to cling, and with mechanical prompting, parted with his elegantly-served dinner. As Mike couldn't keep in his berth because of the rolling, he sat on the floor. He visited the rail and declared that he spat up more than a pint of salt water, and then returning to the stateroom spent the balance of the night in practice with the life preservers. Indeed the steamer rolled very much, frequently throwing down arm chairs that stood on deck, and once pitching a woman from her chair nearly overboard, she being only saved by being thrown against one of the stanchions supporting the upper deck. Cook said in the morning that he was not sick; but later he told how he had sought to ignite the electric burner with a match, and it was concluded that if he was not seasick, he must have been something worse. Everything considered, the first appearance of the party after crossing the Tropic of Cancer indicated a wretched night; and the green fields of Cuba, with the walls of Havana glinting in the morning sunlight, were welcome objects to all.

FIRST GLIMPSES OF HAVANA.

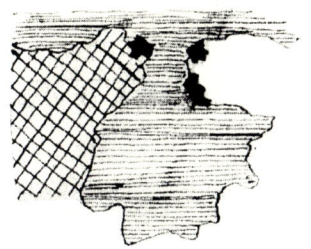
Morro Castle and the Punta forts are at either side of the narrow entrance, and in sixty seconds after turning in from the Gulf of Mexico and passing their frowning guns, the vessel was in the harbor and steaming along the city front as quietly as if a hundred miles from the rolling sea. So sudden was the transition and so rapidly shifted the scene, that all passed like a fleeting vision, leaving the stranger with eyes, ears, and mouth open in the fruitless effort to catch all the novel scenes surrounding him, and so entirely different from those abandoned only a few hours before. The general view of Havana from the deck of the steamer, around whose historic walls cluster so many enchanting memories of the early Spanish discoverers and adventurers, was like a beautiful painting, showing a chimneyless and streetless mass of white Moorish architecture, starting up from the water's edge, and extending toward a few green low and broken hills a couple of miles inland. The shipping included probably not more than fifty craft of all kinds, exclusive of one or two hundred small boats with their sterns covered with hooped awnings. These began to put out from the shores as the "Mascotte" slowly steamed along, and by the time anchor was dropped a half mile inside of Morro, thirty or forty of them were pulling along with the steamers, awaiting the arrival of the customs officers.

These boats were numbered, and bore names indicative of the fancy of their owners, such as "Los Dos Hermanos"; "Los Dos Hermanas"; "Los Amigos"; "Rosarita"; "Las Niñas" etc., and each carried a sail and a pair of oars. They remained a few feet away until the customs officers boarded, and then they scrambled up like cats. The boats mostly belonged to the thinly-clad, swarthy, and broad-chested men who manned them, who made a livelihood by the transportation of passengers on the water. Others were attached to the hotels, and the several interpreters learning that Rendon had already secured the largest party, began to chaff him in broken English, but really intended for his guests. They called out that even if he had seduced travelers into going to the San Carlos he would be unable to keep them more than a day, at which all the boatmen laughed and gave their approval. Of course the travelers understood that they would have said the same of any other hotel that had obtained the passengers, and therefore participated in the enjoyment of the boatmen far more than Rendon did, who seemed to fear that his birds might take fright and fly away. Most of the vessels in the harbor bore the Spanish flag of red and yellow, but one large black cannon-muzzled vessel, with wide square yards, had the majestic heaviness only possessed by the old steamers of the United States Navy, and carried the dear old bunting that thrills the Yankee heart in foreign lands. This vessel was the "Powhatan."

The sun was shining brightly on the water and the buildings; the breeze was a little low and the mercury a little high. The jabbering of fifty Cubans in an unknown tongue, with a succession of solicitations from hotel interpreters presenting their cards, and each giving eager assurance that his was the only first-class house in "Habana"; where all the ship captains and Americans stopped; the only place where no garlic was employed, and where the people spoke "Inglis," all passed too quickly, for Rendon, still not quite certain that some other fellow might not capture his fish after all his anxiety and trouble, hurried them into the "Dos Amigos" as quickly as possible, where for the first time since leaving Jacksonville he heaved an immense sigh of relief and safety. The keys of their trunks, as well as their satchels, were delivered to Rendon, who left a representative of the hotel to see them through the custom house to the San Carlos, and where it may now be said they arrived in an hour without appearance of molestation. The sail was hoisted, and the Dos Amigos was soon at the custom house landing, where Rendon insisted on the ladies carrying their own handbags until the sacred precincts and the guard were passed. They landed at a little flight of stone steps laved by the gentle waves, and were at once greeted by a semi-cripple with lottery tickets, announcing in a drawling voice that the drawing would occur "m-a-ñ-a-n-a." They smiled an American "no," walked past some marines in striped white and blue, their uniforms trimmed with red, who were grouped around a door bearing the arms of Spain and Havana, and were ushered into the streets of the "Key of the New World." The streets were not to exceed 20 or 25 feet in width; paved with small blocks of imported granite; sidewalks four or five inches higher than the pavement, and  from one to three feet wide. They walked arm in arm in the street, and while their eyes devoured the novel sights with intense satisfaction, and a conviction that they had found something that would give them many pleasurable hours, the natives stopped and looked at them with equal gratification, somewhat as Americans formerly stared at the early Chinese immigrants. They had read many accounts of what they should see in Havana, in fact, had crammed for the occasion, but reading is not seeing. "Just look at those oxen yoked by the horns," said Roger. "Yes, and do you mind their big flat feet?" said Mike. "Mercy! What sidewalks!" exclaimed Jane; while Anna took it all in and demanded that Roger should not walk so

fast. Rendon himself seemed to derive satisfaction from their wonder, and victoriously piloted them three or four blocks to a building whose outwards appearance is so well exhibited herewith that further description is unnecessary.

The hotel portion of the Edificio de Luz was up two flights of marble stairs, and Mike and Jane were at once assigned to No. 28, and Roger and Anna to 29, which were connected by folding doors. Rendon informed them that they could have breakfast at nine o'clock, which considering their experience of the preceding night while crossing the Tropic of Cancer, and their having partaken of nothing but a cup of coffee and an orange before leaving the "Mascotte," and some of them not that, was particularly welcome. While awaiting breakfast, the artist unlimbered his pencil and produced the subjoined sketch of the main floor of the hotel where they resided for five weeks:

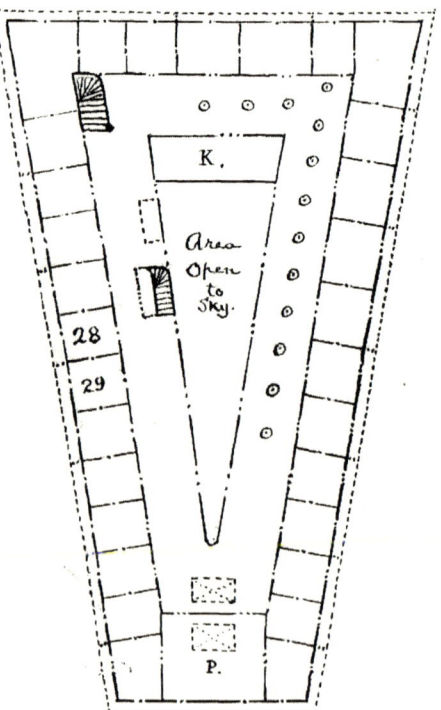

The main stairway and the floor of the hall and all the rooms were laid in marble, which Rendon said was imported from Italy, and was necessary because of the intense heat of summer; while it was useful as well, in ridding the rooms of fleas, being too cold for their comfort. As breakfast was not ready at nine, the artist also sought to make a diagram of rooms 28 and 29, and produced the following:

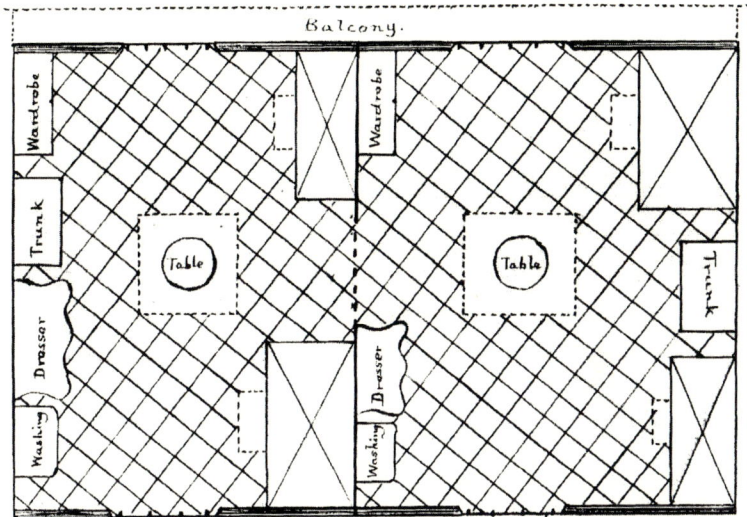

The hotel balcony was protected by an iron railing, and formed a pleasant place from which to view the street, which was about 25 feet wide, and upon the opposite side of which were other balconies adjoining the rooms of families living above the stores. The doors of the rooms were ten to twelve feet high, double, and folding, and painted blue. The inner set of doors were of solid wood, and the outer set of slats. In each half of the former was a little panel door about three feet long and one wide, which could be opened to admit light when the wooden doors were closed. The panels covered glass, which was all the room contained. The double doors permitted the room to be entirely closed, as in windy, rainy, or cold weather, or the heavy folding doors opened and the slat doors closed, as in hot weather. Each room contained a single and double bed, and they were as novel as the wildest imagination could desire—being iron frames, over which stout canvas was tightly drawn. Upon the canvas were two sheets and a thin blanket, while over all, gracefully looped back with bright blue ribbands, were gorgeous mosquito bars. All the rooms were cheaply whitewashed, and had green dados about two and a half feet high.

Hotel Life.

Hotel life at the "Gran San Carlos" was not eventful. They proceeded to their first breakfast with quivering appetites; partly because of their experience the preceding night while crossing the Tropic of Cancer, and partly from the numerous reports by tip and type of the disagreeable character of Cuban cooking. Mr. Rendon had assured them, however, that the San Carlos had very superior cooks, and was free from the objectionable garlic and onions so common in all other Cuban hotels. One round table accommodated the four, reinforced by Mr. Cook; and a short stumpy black-eyed fellow approached with a Spanish bill of fare, which he began to translate into Choctaw English. After listening with aching ears for a few moments, Mike suggested that a breakfast be brought, from which they could determine what best they relished, and order in the future accordingly. Thereupon a long, lank, cross-eyed, dark-skinned hippity-hoppity fellow brought it on—consisting of vino Catalan—a cheap Spanish wine similar to claret, and costing about eight cents a quart bottle—fried eggs, two kinds of fried fish, sweet potato, fried banana, Irish potato, mush, stew, steak, jelly, smear-case, oranges, bananas, bread and coffee. The variety was certainly sufficient, and the quantity ditto. Nearly all of the dishes had been intimately associated with garlic or oil, even to the eggs. The stew was the most wonderful conglomeration of slush that civilized man ever introduced to his stomach, and theirs were too tender to enjoy more than a whiff. Roger knitted his brows and after a moment's study ventured a few words in alleged Spanish at Hippity Hoppity, who brightened like a good fellow as he afterwards proved to be, and who went back at him with two or three yards of rrrrrs, accompanied with many short and quick gestures. He seemed very much disappointed when Roger had to shake his head in token of incomprehension.

The dinner was worse than the breakfast, and to select from it enough that Americans could eat, was like getting a draught of fresh water from middle of the ocean. As Mr. Rendon had frequently expressed the desire that they should make their complaints and wishes known, they soon began to grumble, and little by little their meals became more palatable; but it was not until a week or more, when they returned very hungry from an afternoon's visit to the forts, and found a dinner that they could not eat, that they talked to the point, and assured Mr. Rendon that reform was necessary in order to retain their company. Then they wrote down a few simple wishes that they wanted, which were to be utter strangers to oil or garlic, and after that they were fairly well pleased.

The next morning after their arrival, upon ringing the bell, a short fat old woman appeared at their doors, who readily comprehended their Spanish request for "dos cafés con leche"; and with a "Sí Señor," soon returned with a small silver waiter, with two cups and saucers, a silver pot of hot milk, and its mate with black coffee, a saucer of loaf sugar, and two curious things about the shape of a hunk of something, and the same size, but very much harder, which on breaking, after several attempts, provide to be rolls of bread. These refreshments being partaken "en deshabille" they were succeeded by a short nap, which enabled them to recover from the effects of the efforts at getting inside the biscuits. This became the usual custom with Mike and Jane, while Roger and Anna established the habit of taking their coffee after rising for good. The old lady was familiar with half dressed guests, and was therefore never known to peep through her fingers upon entering.

HOTEL SAN CARLOS.

Propietario: SECUNDINO REBOZO.

ALMUERZO del dia 17 de Enero de 1886.

SOBREMESA.

Jamon E. *ham*
Aceitunas. *olives*
Mantequilla.
Ostras. E. *oysters*

Salchichon E.
Rábanos.
Encurtidos. E.
Queso de puerco.

SOPAS.

Sustancia de gallina. *chicken soup*
Pescado. *fish soup*

VARIOS.

veal chop *mutton chop*
Costilla de carnero.
—Idem de ternera. *ov*
Idem de puerco. *pork*
pigs feet Lomo de puerco frito.
Patas. *alcaparras*
Hígado.

Huevos. *eggs*
Beefsteak.
Picadillo de ternera. *hash*
Mondongo. *tripe*
Carnero. *ragout*
Riñon. *sautée kidneys*
Ensalada de carne. *meat salad*
Butifarras. *sausages*

PESCADOS

Bacalao. *vizcaina*
Almejas. *guisada*
Calamares

A la minuta.
Camarones. E.
Tortas
Sardinas. E.

LEGUMBRES.

Arroz blanco.
Boniatos fritos. *sw. pot.*

Plátanos fritos. *osturoes*
Harina de maiz frita.
frijoles cocidos
potatoes boiled

POSTRES.

preserves + syrups
Dulces en almíbar.
Idem en pasta. *guava jelly*
Frutas en conserva. E.
preserved fruits

Quesos. *cheese*
Frutas de la estacion. *cassava*
queso Neufchatel E

CAFÉ, TÉ Y LECHE.

HOTEL SAN CARLOS.

Propietario: SECUNDINO REBOZO.

COMIDA del día 22 de Enero de 1886

SOPAS.

Juliana.　　　　　　　　　Pan.
Potage de *Garbanzos*　　Arroz *Puré de calabaza*

VARIOS.

Olla española.　　　　　　Ternera asada.
Pollo asado.　　　　　　　Carnero idem.
Idem sauté.　　　　　　　　Frituras de sesos.
Roastbeef.　　　　　　　　Idem de criadillas.
　　　　　　　　　　　　　Menudos de pollo. *Juliana*
　　　　　　　　　　　　　Ternera. *estofada*
Croqueta de ave
Lengua Milanesa

PESCADOS

Frito.　　　　　　　　　　Ostras. E.
A la minuta.　　　　　　　Camarones. E.
El mismo　　　　　　　*Rancho E.*

LEGUMBRES.

Arroz blanco ó amarillo.　　Puré de papas.
Habichuelas verdes.　　　　Boniato asado.
Pimiento relleno　　　　*Papas asadas*

POSTRES.

Dulces en almíbar.　　　　Quesos.
Idem en pasta.　　　　　　Frutas de la estación.
Frutas en conserva. E.
Varios　　　　　　　　　*Queso Neufchâtel*

CAFÉ, TÉ Y LECHE.

NOTAS.

1ª—Los artículos marcados con la letra E son considerados como extras para las personas que coman como Abonados, y por la tanda, si los apetecieren, les serán servidos, cargándoles el importe de tarifa por separado.

2ª—Toda persona que coma en este establecimiento, podrá exigir del dependiente que le sirva, la nota ó carta, por escrito, del gasto que haya hecho.

3ª—Los comensales Abonados solo podrán tomar como incluido en el abono, el vino tinto conocido generalmente por Vino catalán; si tomaren de cualquiera otra clase de los enumerados en la tarifa de vinos, impresa por separado, se les cargará también por separado y como extra en el importe fijado.

4ª—El dueño de este establecimiento agradecerá á sus favorecedores cualquiera observacion que le dirijan respecto á faltas cometidas en el servicio ó quejas de otra especie, que sean justas, á las cuales pondrá inmediatamente el más eficáz correctivo.

Imp. S. Ignacio 38.

Being in a country where sleeping rooms could be left open for a free passage of air, and supposing it to be desirable to employ all the appliances provided, Mike and Jane slept for a few nights with only the blinds closed, but soon abandoned it until downright hot weather, while Roger and Anna always slept bottled up.

After rising it was customary to take a Victoria or a walk to some point of interest until ten or eleven o'clock, and then return for breakfast, which consisted first of a pared orange stuck upon a fork which served as a handle, and from which the orange was gnawed. It was delicious eating—all melting into the mouth but the core, and the fork. A bottle of wine was always at hand, but Mike and the ladies soon swore off, because some one said it was not well to partake of fruit after wine. Then came broiled red snapper, very excellent, with Irish and sweet potatoes, accompanied by lettuce, water cress and little tomatoes. The fish was always accompanied by four nice fried eggs, or green pea omelette, together with fried bananas, fried sweet potatoes, and fried corn mush. Then came chops or a steak tenderloin, always nice, followed by dessert, consisting of guava jelly or paste, preserved citron, shredded pineapple, granulated cocoanut, fresh pineapple and cheese. Mike always smacked his lips when Switzer took the place of the decent kind. Finally coffee and toothpicks, and two or three oranges for the pocket, with which "Domingo" sometimes, after a fee, hippity-hopped around to the room. After breakfast the ladies would adjourn to the balcony facing the water, to watch the milkmen under an Alamo tree wash their milk cans, and speculate upon which they would have if they resided in Havana. Anna selected one with white pants and shirt, but Jane was never able to make a choice. The men took a smoke, and after wandering an hour returned for a nap on the feather beds, which by that time had been vacated by the ladies. Between four and five, after a midday tour in which all participated, if crib would permit, they strolled around the triangle for dinner. This consisted of wine, lettuce, water cress, tomatoes, as in the morning; soup of various denominations, sometimes saffron and vermicelli, and at others of chicken necks or an indescribable composition which they never assaulted. None of the soups were much sought for. The very sight of the big dried peas floating around in a sea of oil gravy was sea sickening. The slices of fish fried to a golden yellow, either with or without lime juice, were very fine. This was followed by roast chicken or a quartette of little birds, with their legs curled up over their bellies in a piteous way, resting their backs in a soft bedding of mashed potatoes. Then came roast tenderloin six or eight inches long with boiled sweet and Irish potatoes, followed by a similar dessert to the morning. After dinner a tour to some part of the city ensued for an hour or two, or the evening was whiled away with crib or dominoes until ten o'clock, when all retired to their little beds.

One day a priest and his assistant came to forgive the sins of an old man of ninety in the room adjoining Cook's. The priest's boy was armed with a silver candlestick and a club, and his attendant with a great lantern to illuminate the old man's room that had been darkened to exclude the world and all thoughts of it. Mike and Roger suspended cribbage during the exercises, not so much from religious respect for the cloth, or for an old man of ninety who, having galloped through a life of errors, was at the last moment beseeching Heaven for pardon, but rather from curiosity to note the sorrow on the countenance of the priest after such a solemn scene, and observe again his garb and paraphernalia. As five minutes sufficed for the confession Mike and Roger concluded that if he, being ninety years old, had entered upon a detailed statement, he must have been an exceptionally good man, which was furthered evidenced by the priest who withdrew in a smiling mood, and laughed and chatted gaily on his way to the stairway—a great tall awkward man clad in very dirty vestments, with doubtless a handsome fee in his pocket.

Numerous visits were made to the roof of the hotel to scan the heavens for the long-heard-of "Southern Cross," none of the party having ever before been far enough South; but after many fruitless visits and inquiries they finally concluded that the Cross was invisible at that latitude until later in the season. Once Roger induced the ladies to break up an exciting game of dominoes to make the usual heavenly observations and dwell on the beauties of the evening, but on their ascent the rain began to fall and they only saw the "Mascotte" steaming out with her well-lighted decks, and a small balloon in the sky floating northward to the United States. When crib, dominoes and all else palled, the men were accustomed to take the roof, where after a few times round they recited some of their adventures in the war, and told how such and such a gigantic enterprise should have been conducted. Military science was the loser by having no representative present to jot down the words of wisdom that trickled from their lips by the side of their Havanas.

The balcony in front of their rooms was a pleasant resort for an hour, either morning or evening; but Roger complained that as soon as he put in an appearance the fleas waiting in the street below instantly began their ascent. Some climbed the side of the house, and some crawling up the building over the way balanced across the street on the wires. Others yet, particularly active and hungry, jumped. These pests made it lively for George and Jane, but never molested Mike. Roger complained of sleepless nights on their account, and finally took to bay rum baths before retiring, and then rolling in a sheet. To illustrate, however, how nature makes all things even, Mike lost his watch twice in a remarkable manner; and Anna was laid up with a sick ear so that Dr. Finley of Compostella street was called in.

Across the way from the balcony was a parrot in a tailor shop, and he talked, laughed, cussed, and wept in Spanish. At times he so mimicked a crying child as to cause the family portion of the party serious inconvenience.

One day from the balcony they all gathered to witness a battle between a dog and a cock on the street below. The dog was little and yellow, and the cock big and red. The latter pushed the fight with relentless vigor, bristling his feathers, ducking his head, making feints at the dog and then flying up to spur him in the face and eyes. The dog on the other hand seemed to be convulsed with laughter. He danced all around, barking incessantly, and occasionally pouncing upon him seized the cock by the neck and held him down upon the pavement for a minute or so. While thus held the cock made no struggles to get free, but as soon as released would again bristle up and renew the fight. This they continued for a half hour, the cock exhibiting genuine pluck and courage and the dog a love of sport; until finally the latter ran playfully around the corner, the cock following as defiant as ever.

As time was occasionally a trifle tedious joking was always in order, and in which the entire circle joined. Rendon himself possessed a vein of humor, and related how at Jacksonville he had told a traveler that two suppers were provided at the hotel, the principal one being at ten o'clock. The traveler having scorned the cheap six o'clock affair hung around with increasing impatience until 10:30, and then roused Rendon from sleep to know where the ten o'clock supper was set. "Ten o'clock" gradually came to be used as a comment when a doubtful statement was ventured, or when anyone taking them for tenderfeet endeavored to stuff them with improbabilities.

The "ten o'clock" story reminds the historian of the ancient time-piece which hung upon a column at the parlor end of the long hallway. It never rang the hour without suggesting that solemn period when Life will be loosening its grip, and the grim Reaper tightening his bony fingers around the heart strings. Every stroke seemed a gasp for which all its energies were gathered; and at midnight, when tormented with sleeplessness, it seemed nearly one o'clock before the last stroke of twelve.

Mrs. Warner was the only resident lady of Havana speaking English, whose acquaintance was made, and when she called in black lace veil and saluted the ladies upon both cheeks, in Cuban style, Mike whispered to Roger that it would not look well for her to return alone and he would therefore accompany her home to see the baby. Roger claimed that Mike took an unfair advantage, and was like the western schoolboy who raised his hand in the middle of the afternoon and obtained the handsome teacher's consent to see her home, before the other boys had a chance; but the taunt had no effect beyond a repetition from Mike that he was only going to see the baby.

Just at one end of the hotel began the Alameda de Paula, an attractive promenade by the sea wall, and along which the party sometimes strolled. At the farther extremity were the remains of an old stone fort, with a little round watch tower at one angle, through the narrow slits of which it was presumed many generations ago the bucklered sentinel peered forth in stormy weather to catch the first glimpse of the invading pirate and smuggler. With historic interest Anna climbed the wall one morning and paraded in the footsteps of the old sentinels.

One morning the Havana ambassador to the Court of Madrid landed from a steamer, and a large crowd of gentlemen received him at the remote end of the Paula, while the Denver party waited on the balcony by the parlor. The crowd marched along the Paula to the hotel, with a brass band, and filled the parlor and reception room with excited Cubans, after which they had a speech of welcome and a reply. Mike and Roger witnessed the speeches by looking in a large mirror opposite, which reflected their features and their gestures. Then the crowd destroyed a large quantity of wine and dirtied the marble floors.

The ambassador's sister, a heavy-weight Cuban belle, seemed borne down by the moral responsibility of being related to the gentleman receiving the reception—like the old Revolutionary lady whose husband was appointed Corporal. The meeting of the ambassador and his male friends was followed by their arms being flung around each other for a few seconds, and perhaps a few pats on the back, but nothing like such an embrace as an American is apt to be acquainted with under the name of a "hug."

One morning an old photographer appeared and pictured the dining room and building. He explained that he was not feeling very well, because he had just been photographing a man whom the doctors had cut up, and it had made him sort of sick. The party went upon the porch at the north end of the building and looked excessively pretty during the operation, but alas! the view of each was only the size of a mosquito's eye, and their prettyness did not appear. He or she who reads these records will understand, however, that with a very powerful microscope the result would be quite different. Mike and Roger were anxious for a general view of Havana, and engaged the old fellow to take such a one from the San Carlos roof, and for which they paid him fifteen dollars paper.

On the 14th of February at the breakfast table the ladies found a beautiful illustrated valentine beneath each of their plates, which caused them to partake heartily of cucumbers which appeared that morning for the first time. Jane's missive was prefaced with a picture of a glass eye, followed by the accompanying stanza:

"Dear lady with the kind blue eye.
"More lovely than a piece of pie:
"(Which while in Cuba with its cooks,
"Expresses more than first it looks)
"Give me but one glance of thine,
"And evermore thy Valentine."

Anna's love ditty was also touchingly sentimental, and pitiful, too, being modestly introduced by a spirited drawing of a full-grown heart pierced by a cruel arrow, and beneath it inscribed the following tender lines:

"Lady, here's my punctured heart,
"More clinging than the vine.
"Please put it in its little bed,
"And I will be your Valentine."

During the approaching last days at Havana Roger took a spasm of writing during most of his spare time, and the other three played dominoes, the ladies usually alleging that Mike cheated them. When the ladies played by themselves and the game was blocked, each counted all she had left in her hand. They said the game progressed more rapidly in that way.

ON THE SAN CARLOS ROOF.

By ascending one flight of stairs from the main floor the first roof of the San Carlos was reached, that part covering the row of rooms represented on the diagram. Above the triangular hall which served as office, reception room and dining room, arose another story, the roof of which could be mounted from the first. These roofs were flat, and covered with square red tile set in cement like a marble floor. The first was protected by a thick wall some three feet high, encompassing an area of about 700 feet by 25. One of the chief sources of enjoyment of an evening was to ascend to this roof, and arm in arm promenade around the block, (for the streets surrounded the building on all sides) or seated in rockers by the wall enjoy the beauties of the heavens and the harbor.

Off to the North, over the low tile-clad roofs of intervening buildings, blazed the intermittent Morro light, telling of a rocky coast and informing the mariner leagues away in the Gulf as clearly his whereabouts on the trackless wave as if he stood reading the names on the street corners of Havana. A little to the right, and in nearer and clearer view, frowned in the moonlight the high walls of the fortress of San Carlos de la Cabañas, and it almost seemed as if the tread of the sentinel could be heard pacing back and forth as had been continuously done for generations. Below the Cabañas, near the water's edge, glinted the bright lights of Casa Blanca; and further to the right the more numerous jets of Regla and her sugar houses, with red, white and green eyes, marking the ferry boat slips. In and about all this floated the lanterns at the fore on all the shipping, with here and there a moving spark showing the entrance or departure of craft. Below in the brilliantly illuminated triangular park known as the "Plaza de Luz," from a Marquis once owning the land thereabouts, and along by the Alameda de Paula, ranged forty or fifty Victorias, with others constantly arriving or departing. The warning tap of the bell on the approach of the ferry boats to the slips was always followed by a dozen or more Victorias scampering across the pavement with their rattling wheels and rattled horses, to post across the way so as to secure passengers by obstructing the exit. Soldiers or the Civil Guard, with the sleeves of their scarlet-trimmed uniforms bandaged in crepe in respect to the memory of the lately deceased King of Spain, marched hither and thither as if ever on the trail of an insurgent or a peace-breaker. Vestless, coatless and shirtless men of all colors but unadulterated white lounged beneath the arches, or in the stores, saloons and living rooms across the Plaza de Luz. On the west a sea of tile presented its thousand faces to the gaze, relieved by rugged irregularity, and an occasional church tower, half in shade, pointing the way that so few in Havana sought to travel. On the nearer roofs across the Calle de Oficios, which appeared not difficult to leap, a few dim lights denoted the retreat of men and women from the lower and busier quarters to the coolness of the rooms above. Softly treading along the tiles were cats—which with cocks and dogs seemed as natural to Cuban soil as darkeys and fleas. Leaning over the wall and looking out upon the tiles around, cats were in front, cats on the right, cats on the left, cats and kittens at their feet, and cats as far as the eye could reach in the darkness. By day they lay in the doorways, on the counters, in the windows, among the groceries, on the cigarettes, beneath the shady eaves, behind the thin curtains, and on the flower tubs in the inner courts. Afar in the background on the one hand loomed the castle of Atares, within whose precincts it was said were shot the young American Crittenden and his fifty comrades, who with greater hearts than heads sought to aid Cuban freedom, but only gave to a relentless monarchy their hopeful lives. In the opposite direction towered the Cathedral which boasts of holding the ashes of him who gave this content to a greedy world. Over and above all in the deep blue vault sparkled the silvery stars as beautifully and in the same eternity of fixedness as when they guided the intrepid mariner in his little "Santa Maria" across the unknown sea to the then peaceful Cuban shores. Sometimes in the dark of the moon the stars and the lights on the shipping sent their beams reflecting along the quiet water like a narrow flight of silver stairs emborded with walls of inky black. By day the scene in the Plaza de Luz was somewhat more monotonous in the bright sunshine, but in the harbor the canvas-covered sail boats skipped along in the never-ending breeze; the "Guanabacoa," the "Edouard Fesser" and the "Maria Isabel" plied from shore to shore, the shipping gaily floated its red and yellow bunting of blood and gold, but the stars and stripes were conspicuous by their absence.

LETTERS OF INTRODUCTION.

The writer has seen statements in certain books of travel that letters of introduction to Cubans were only so much waste paper, and that because the Havana business men received so many they were bluff and uncivil to the bearers. The experience of the party was to the contrary, but possibly their eminently respectable appearance had much to do with their reception. After calling on American Consul General Williams, and who returned their call on the following Sunday while they were engaged at the Plaza de Toros, they took the forenoon of January 18th to deliver their letters. Dr. Erastus Wilson, at 115 Prado, occupied extensive quarters of three stories and numerous rooms, tastefully adorned with choice works of art from various parts of the world he had visited, and who showed among his possessions a thirteen-hundred dollar dog in its old age, and an American billiard table. He was an American bachellor of considerable intelligence, who upon mention of the possibility of their taking rooms in private quarters, offered them two of his own at four ounces ($68.00) per month oro. His residence was a type of all of the better class—a severely plain front with wide double-doored entrance for a carriage and horses, through which were visible the stable and a small court garnished with exotics. The stairway of marble to the living rooms and office, started from the carriage way and not from the street. His tiled roof formed a small promenade, where the beauties of the sky and the thousand gas jets of the Prada might be enjoyed while gently rocking to and fro and wafting away the smoke from fragrant Havanas. Much interesting information was obtained from Dr. Wilson, and the party lost much in this respect by not taking his rooms. On one occasion, when there was still a prospect of this, and he was therefore a caller at the San Carlos until eleven at night, he said the country Cubans were brokenhearted because at the last revolution the United States had not espoused their cause and declared war against Spain. He thought there was no hope for Cuban independence except through the United States. The Spanish officials were squeezing the people dry so that they were unable to pay their taxes, and their lands and houses were therefore rapidly being confiscated. He said that the Spaniards were thus coming into possession of the property, and thought when they had secured the major part, the terrible taxation would terminate. He appeared to think it had for its object the enrichment of a Spanish clique at the expense of the native Cubans, between whom was no sympathy. He cited the case of an $80,000 residence that was in the market at $15,000. His advice to strangers was to take the middle of the street when out after dark and carry few valuables. If attacked he recommended the killing of the assailant but to represent to the authorities that the man had run against their knives. He carried a sword cane himself, and cheered them with stories of robbery by daylight in the public streets, a division of the spoils with the unpaid civil guard, and consequent impossibility of recovery if attempted. The Doctor was a Mason, and advised them to let the Havana brethren alone, claiming that their masonry was solely for what they could make from it, and that they entertained none of those moral ideas which are professed by the fraternity in the United States. They concluded to adopt his advice, and therefore the only tokens of Masonry that they saw was a sign or two like "The Voice of Hiram," and a saddle that attracted attention in the doorway of a store. It was very old and covered with silver filigree work. On the pommel was a silver square and compass some three inches square, with a solid golden "G" in the center.

At 9 1/2 O'Reilly street, which Americans pronounce in the usual O'Rily manner, and the Cubans call O'Ralye or O'Rilya, they found Señor Francisco P. Alvarez, a young man of twenty-six, who by the death of his father a month before had become the proprietor of the largest cigar factory in Cuba. He pressed some samples upon the visitors, and engaged to meet them the next morning at the factory. At No. 8, Calle de Tacon, they met a Cubanized German wearing the name of Kicherer. He was in

the commission business, was very cordial, offered his services for anything that was desired, and subsequently became their banker for the cashing of drafts. He gave them advice free, such as to beware of drafts of air and avoid sunshine and moonshine. The latter idea being new to Mr. Cook he was somewhat alarmed, and lost no opportunity of inquiring of others if the danger was very great, and what precautions had better be employed. Kicherer said that the moonlight being much stronger than in the States its effect was bad, but on being pressed by Roger to illustrate, he failed the respond satisfactorily, and they bade him good morning with the remark that it was about "ten o'clock" and they must leave.

Dr. Joseph Warner was a young Massachusetts dentist, who resided and practiced at 79 O'Reilly, with the entrance around the corner. He was a little man with a Cuban born American wife, who desired to return to the United States after coming into possession of muchos pesos. The Doctor was fond of sport, and spent every Sunday in the country with his dog and gun. Mrs. Warner said that as he was taxed $22.50 a year for the privilege of carrying a fowling piece, he hunted all the way back to the depot. His dog was all the property he had that was free from tax. Mrs. Warner had met other Denver people in Havana, so that besides giving the ladies some highly interesting information concerning Cuban domestic life, she was good company generally. Among other gossip she related how Billy Wilson the preceding winter had the Havana people convulsed at his ludicrous errors in dancing, when he insisted on gaily participating without being acquainted with the steps.

Señor Ricardo Kohly was a busy importer who suspended his studies of correspondence to give a kindly greeting, and who tendered letters of introduction to sugar planters, by which they might obtain egress to the wonders of a factory. Without exception, all to whom they bore letters received and treated them kindly, and without making it appear laborious either.

STREET SCENES.

The street scenes in Havana were exceedingly novel to the Americans from the moment of putting foot on shore. First were the narrow streets, and the barred openings in lieu of windows, giving every house the appearance of a prison. The store doors were open, which with the barred window places exposed pretty much the whole front. The stores were small and crowded with goods. Very many of the people on the streets wore a thin undershirt, possibly open at the breast, light pants, small boots, or shoes or slippers down at the heel and the heel sticking out. The heavy carts were drawn by mules or oxen. The latter were of good size, first rate condition, a native breed colored like the Jersey, except the head and legs were quite dark, and were yoked by the horns, sometimes tandem, or a pair to a pole, or one in heavy shafts. The heads of the animals were held as if in a vise, while the tremor of the wheels in passing over the pavement was conveyed through the shafts or tongue to their imprisoned heads, giving them a perpetual quiver. They were guided by rope reins passing through the cartilage of the nostrils. Some of the narrow business streets were crossed by iron rods, over which awnings were drawn by ropes, permitting a walk of perhaps a quarter of a mile at a time protected from the bright light and heat. The stores rarely showed the names of the proprietors, but had fancy names without the slightest reference to the nature of the business. Roger and Mike went out copying names one day, and selected such as: "La Marina"; "Café y billar"; "Fonda y posada tres hermanos"; "El correo de las Antilles"; "La Granada Reformada"; "La Lealtad"; "La Engina"; "Café el Infante"; "La Imparcial"; "Glorieta Cubana"; "La Calla de Sant Mus"; "El Dedal de Oro"; "El Gallo"; "El Brazo Fuerte"; "La Bella Habanera"; "La Josefina"; "La Fama"; "El Correo de Nueva York"; "El Fuerte del Cristo"; "Palo Gordo"; "Modelo de Viena"; "El Dos de Mayo"; "Fonda el Sol de Madrid". The pawnbroker's sign of "Casa de Prestamos" was a frequent object, and the residences of rich and poor were in close juxtaposition. The houses at street corners bore inscription of

"Subida" or "Bajada," indicating whether vehicles were permitted to be driven down or up. A barber's sign was a picture of a pair of shears and the figures "40"; and a razor with the figures "30." It was said that this originated in an effort to tax all public signs five cents per letter, and Mrs. Warner said that the Doctor had to pay $3.00 per year for his doorplates and dental signs. The beggars in the streets are wonderful specimens of the human frame divine, are of all hues but white, and of both sexes. One woman sits on the sidewalk in Mercaderes street with a bare leg lying on the sidewalk in front of her that she is no more able to carry along than if she was an infant. It was wobbled and twisted and swollen and creased so that none could imagine what it was were it not for the body attached. One man stationed on Obispo street literally dragged his long lank body along the ground when moving, and whom it would seem to be a mercy to shoot through the head. A Chinaman in the same neighborhood daily sat with his back to the building and occupying the entire width of the sidewalk, though drawn up in the smallest possible compass. Traveling beggars were everywhere beheld, some at the church doors, mute in their appeals, but usually brazen. The Americans wondered why they were thus permitted to advertise the indisposition of the people to care for the helpless in an organized way, unless a revenue was derived from taxing the privilege of begging. One unfortunate fellow with both legs and one arm amputated always sat in a little wagon near the Cristina market. One without feet walked about on his knees soliciting aid in a modest sort of way, and seemed to be doing better than most of the people who were whole. The city seemed to be speckled with deformed persons, even the naked children in the streets showing a neglect that would make them cripples in after years. An interesting local sight was the bathing of horses in the surf at La Punta or along the gulf shore toward Vedada. A man with only a piece of grimy cloth around his loins, or wearing drawers instead, would mount a horse, to the tail of which might be tied another, and still another to that, and soon to a dozen or twenty, and ride into the surf until nothing was visible but the horses' heads and the man, and over which the waves would roll if the animals did not rise with them.

After a few minutes in deep water they would return to shoaled places when the man would dismount and scrub them. The horses appeared to enjoy it, and the men seemed to think baths good for their live stock if not for themselves. Street pedling was common, from the lottery-ticket vendor to a boot and shoe or crockery store on horseback. They have immense saddles made principally of straw, twelve or fifteen inches thick at the cantle, upon which they arrange a variety of methods of transporting truck and wares. They have a long grass flexible basket, like an immense pair of saddle-bags, that lying over the saddle reaches below the horse's belly on each side, and covers the greater part of the horse's body in length. In this they stow away six or eight bushels of corn, beets, peas, live chickens, oranges, and so on, and retail it at the markets or even the streets. One will have eight or ten large milk cans; another on each side of his horse two large coops of two or three stories, containing a hundred or more chickens. Others carry immense loads of green corn fodder, packed lengthwise on the back and sides of the muzzled horse, reaching to within a few inches of the ground, and absolutely nothing visible of the horse but the nose and tail. To the latter a second horse, similarly laden, might be tied, and to that a third, until five or six would be stringing along, nose to tail, like so many animated stacks of corn fodder, all in the care of one man, riding perhaps high in the air upon the forward load. This fodder they retail out, a feed here and another there, as wanted, and which is often fed upon the pavement. Some horses are saddled with wooden cabinets with shelves and glass doors, in which are carried dry goods, boots and shoes, crockery, etc. There are also many foot pedlars with stocks of sweets, tin ware, crockery, etc., on their heads, each having a peculiar call by which he is recognized. The crockery man for instance, goes along with a couple of plates or saucers in one hand, which with his fingers he constantly clacks together. Strings of two, three, or a half dozen cows may be seen slowly straggling along, with their muzzled calves. One cow stops at a house door, where the driver milks a tumbler of milk and froth for the occupants, and passes onto the next customer with his herd. If a cow thinks its calf is being robbed it may become sufficiently intemperate as to induce the driver to unmuzzle the calf and give it five minutes at lunch, after which the old lady plods along again peacefully. The natural tendency to defraud is sometimes illustrated in this method of distributing milk, as it is related that cases have been known in which the milkman held a small sponge in his hand and suffered a little water therefrom to trickle down the cow's teat into the tumbler. The asses are also milked from door to door, and the numerous goats that illustrate the vacant lots of the city look as if they ought to be. The milkman and the goats having passed, here comes a funeral—a black hearse with two or four black horses, their long black trappings trimmed extensively with gold—a driver with cocked hat and coat front glittering with golden braid, as if the hero of a hundred battles. Four or six pall-bearers in liveried coats on a somewhat less gorgeous style than the driver, and carriages following in the rear, containing men only, complete the scene. A half hour later comes down the same street a more humble funeral. Four negroes, naked to the waist, carry the coffin, rented for this particular occasion—two at the head side by side, with their inside arms about each other, and two at the foot in the same manner, with the coffin on the bare shoulders of the two couples, who speed along so rapidly that the half dozen straggling followers keep on a dog trot, the widow amongst the rest. Small squads of soldiers are frequently met in the streets, and when the relief guard makes its round, one rank occupies the sidewalk on one side, and the other the other. Pedestrians who meet them have the privilege of the street. The few store wagons are generally covered. Freight is handled in high two-wheeled heavy carts, drawn by a single mule or one or two oxen. The mules are small, but generally well-conditioned and well-shaped—rounded and smooth. Their loads are heavy for smoothly-worn granite pavements, and sometimes they start with much difficulty. In one such instance the driver was seen to take the mule's head in both arms, when holding and steadying it as if in a vise, the animal was enabled to succeed. These carts will often be seen drawn up alongside the narrow sidewalks, the mules munching corn fodder from the pavement, and the drivers on their backs or bellies in the carts, fast asleep, awaiting jobs. Ladies claiming to belong to first class society never appear in the public streets, on foot. If they go shopping, they sit in their carriages at the door and the goods are brought to them. They are either bareheaded or wear lace veils upon the head, but not covering the face. One morning Mike and Roger with Kicherer visited the Board of Trade, near the old Europa building on Caballeria wharf where Dr. Kane died. A good many men were promenading the cement floor, trying to do business, some with papers of rice in their hands, and others without samples. One man with very tight boots patiently attracted Mike's attention, and who turned out to be a broken down stock gambler, who though ruined in purse, health, and feet, could not keep away from the fire, but took his daily promenade up and down the room during the business hours. On their way to this meeting the men wandered to the sea wall near Empedrado street, and stopped to see a man and his little girl drowning seven young kittens. The young girl seemed to hugely enjoy the sport of throwing them into the water, and seeing them swim, and struggle, and die. Query for the reader: Is this youthful enjoyment a hereditary result of that moral tone consequent upon bull fighting; or is the taste a natural one that with maturer years develops into a passion for bull fighting? Which is the cause and which the effect—which the dog and which the tail?

Modes of Travel.

The narrow streets of Havana, so built because of the necessity of cramping the area to be enclosed with expensive walls, were mostly paved with blocks of granite, some six inches square and others twelve. Some of the sidewalks were in places not to exceed a foot in width, and rarely over three. They were a great nuisance when the party went walking as they had to go in single file or one retain the sidewalk while the other took the street. When the gentlemen were by themselves they frequently took the middle of the street, or kept crossing from side to side upon meeting other pedestrians. Roger could get along pretty well on the narrow sidewalks, but after having fattened on Spanish pie and soup for a week or two Mike's belly swelled so, that he was obliged to occupy the street, and Roger followed out of sympathy. They wore away about an inch from the bottoms of their canes while tramping the paved streets of Havana, hence it may be inferred that walking was inferior to that found on the plains. While the streets were wide enough for carriages to pass, they were too narrow for hasty promiscuous travel, hence some were set apart for passage in one direction, and others the opposite. There were said to be 5,000 Victorias in Havana, the drivers of which paid the owners seven dollars per day paper for the use, feed, and care of the teams. These vehicles seemed to equal in number all other kinds combined, and were sometimes seen by the hundred. They were low-wheeled, and the top shut well down in front affording complete protection from the hot sun or rain. Cubans never rode with the top down, and it was said smiled to see Americans adopt the reverse, as they frequently did. The Victorias were sometimes supplied with two seats, but the front one in such instances was uncomfortable for one, and more so for two. The drivers were Cubans and negroes, and preferred to sleep at the corners than to solicit custom. Were it the custom for them to practice the latter, life in Havana would be insupportable except after dark.

 A Victoria was drawn by a single horse, small, but speedy if in good condition. Many of them, however, were just ready for the bull ring, and their victorias were as aged and dilapidated as they. There were several lines of street cars, the tariff on which varied from ten to twenty cents paper, according to distance. An improvement on cars in the United States were the iron arms or divisions in the seats, rendering it impossible to crowd seated passengers. A span of horses, with an extra one as leader, constituted the motive power, and the driver carried a long-lashed whip which was frequently brought into use. One line of street cars was pulled by dummy engines; and there were also a few vehicles like the diligence of European countries. The volantes which a few years ago filled the streets of the city, and in which the best society appeared in the cool hours of the day, had all given place, with one exception, to the shorter and easier-handled Victoria. In Matanzas a few had been retained for the use of strangers in going over the rough and rocky road to the Caves of Bellamar. The volante was declared to be the only cosa de Cuba of native invention, and it consisted of two large heavy wheels; shafts sixteen feet long reaching only to the shoulders of the horse; a couple leather springs like those of a Concord coach; and a seat with a chaise cover that could be let down, placed midway between the wheels and the horse. There were shafts for one horse, and upon him sat the "calesero," or upon a second animal by its side, attached to the vehicle by a pair of long traces, and the calesero holding the bridle of the harnessed horse. The sensation in a volante was decidedly agreeable, and even when bumping over rocks a foot or more in diameter the motion was of such a rocking nature that it was not unpleasant. The entire length of the vehicle and horse was from twenty to twenty-four feet, and the horse being some eight or ten feet in advance of the wheels permitted him to pass over obstructions completely and be on other footing before the arrival of the wheels at the bad places. The steam cars consisted of three classes, the seats in the cheapest being merely wooden benches without backs. No colored persons were allowed in first class cars, the seats of which were perforated wood or cane, but smoking was common, as in all public vehicles. Among the printed rules for the government of passengers the following will illustrate a Cuban weakness: "Animals are not permitted in first class coaches unless it be a cock in a sack, for a passenger. In other coaches muzzled dogs and six hens are allowed by paying freight." The starting of trains was announced by the ringing of a dinner bell by a colored trainman. The roads were in good condition, rock-ballasted, and the trains run 25 or 30 miles an hour. The ferry boat slips were just across the Plaza de Luz from the hotel. The boats were similar to those of the United States of small capacity, with one side for whites and the other for "personas de color." Other transportation in the harbor was readily secured through some of the numerous sail and row boats for a few cents, or by the hour at an agreed price. There was usually a good breeze and rowing consequently uncalled for.

TALKING SPANISH.

The historian enters upon a short chapter descriptive of the exploits of the several members of the party in employing the Spanish language, with many misgivings of his ability to do the subject full justice in English. The gentlemen had taken about a dozen lessons in Spanish before departing from Denver, but had not been so perfect in their recitations as they would have expected their boys to be in school because they "did not have to"; but what little they did know, was not only serviceable, but enabled them to shine in the society of Americans who knew none, and who stared at the signs painted on the buildings, and wondered what they were all about. Even the ladies shone with reflected brilliancy by being associated with a party that knew so much. At first the gentlemen sought to throw around the San Carlos all the Spanish with which they were possessed, but there being so many that talked broken English the necessity soon appeared minus, and they gradually desisted. Yet Mike kept up a continues flirtation with old Isabel the chamber maid, who waddled like a duck, and was fair, fat, and fifty; and at all hours of the day and evening could be heard his insinuating appeal for "poco frio." If he sat reading or smoking or meditating at one end of the long tiled office, and the black-eyed Isabel appeared around the corner at the other, he was restless and watchful until he had attracted her attention, and expressed the wish for "poco frio en veinte y ocho." When the old lady entered either of the rooms in the performance of her duty, morning, noon, or night, her conversation with the ladies was always instructive and delightful. Isabel ever had an interesting remark in Spanish, to which the ladies would smile and return a "yes" or a "no," or give back some broken baby English on another subject entirely, and thereupon the conversation would run on, each in her own tongue, and unconscious of what the other was saying, but nevertheless just as if all was understood and connected. These conversations were interspersed with numerous expressive smiles and nods and gestures by which it was stoutly maintained that all was perfectly intelligible; and for fear of family discord it is to be understood that no real doubt is here cast upon the claim.

One day when Hippity-Hoppity was taking a plate of fruit to Roger's room in advance of the latter, and hesitated at the door, Roger to assure him that he could proceed without impropriety called out "entre," but Hippity-Hoppity appeared so disconcerted that Roger concluded there was something wrong, and as soon as alone looked up the meaning of "entre." Having ascertained that instead of enter it meant "between," he no longer wondered that Hippity-Hoppity was disconcerted, for he must have thought that Roger intended him to be so impartial in the distribution of the fruit that he should go through the wall between the doors of the two rooms. Nephew Fuller before leaving the San Carlos distinguished himself on several occasions, and as a fine of four cents was imposed on every error, a large fund would have been realized had there been any way to collect it. Where nephew Fuller heard a new word he immediately made a note of it in his memorandum book and immediately forgot what it was, so that when attempting its repetition he invariably manufactured one that was as ludicrous as his English, when one evening in the Sonoro restaurant he grandly informed the party, that the Cuban "resurrection" started in that place a few years before. Any misunderstanding or dispute between either of the party and the natives was settled in English on one side and Spanish on the other; as when the ladies and Roger rode home from the bull fight the driver demanded "dos pesos," and Roger gave him a dollar and a half, to which he objected. Roger told him in English that if he didn't want it he was not obliged to keep it, and held out his hand for its return but the fellow refusing to let go, Roger left him still airing his Spanish. One day when Mike was out alone and losing no opportunity to learn Spanish, he was accosted by an old negro woman at the door of her dwelling, who with the assistance of two mulattos sought to make him give them ten cents to buy coffee with. Mike being ignorant of the proper Spanish for a punched head was obliged to use pure English. As a rule the Cubans could readily understand the party's Spanish, but their replies were so rapid, and the ear so untrained to the sounds, that before recognition they had passed from memory. Ability to speak and understand Spanish would add greatly to the pleasure of a Cuban visit, and give the stranger much more importance among the people. On the other hand ignorance is also sometimes serviceable, as when going where not allowed. Ignorance of language and rules forms a good excuse, and an explanatory shrug or two, with a few deprecatory English words, permits a graceful withdrawal.

MARKETS AND RESTAURANTS.

The stranger to a tropical clime dreams in fancy of lying all day in a hammock beneath a shady bower, and wading stomach-deep during his few waking moments in the luxurious productions of the generous soil—hence an early visit was made to the markets and restaurants to test the reality. Cafés appeared on every hand, where cooling drinks could be obtained for a few inches of paper money. While the ladies were resting the first day the three men strolled slowly through some of the narrow streets, and upon tiring, entered a cheap-looking café, one side of which was adorned with many colored pictures of bullfighting scenes. Calling for "dos limonadas" the keeper presented immense tumblers containing about a quart of water each, tempered with green lime juice and a little sugar. Mike suggested that a Cuban lemonade partook too much of the character of the paper money—more bulk than value. Cook desired ale in preference to a lemonade, and searched his book for the right word after they had all made an attempt to explain to the keeper. At another place they requested cocoanut milk, and taking an immense nut enclosed in the green outer bark, the keeper slashed off the end, and turning it over a goblet filled the latter with the colorless fluid—one nut to a glass. Its mild sweetish taste was hardly palatable to stomachs long accustomed in America to more deadly liquids.

An early visit to the Cristina market revealed a square one-story building, the center being a court either open or shielded from the sun by canvas—the building itself being divided into little stores or stalls opening at one end upon the street and the other upon the court. The odor of the place was distinctly Cuban, and it contained a profusion of fish, flesh, fowl, fruit and vegetables. The fish and flesh presented no new features. The fowls were either alive or dissected, and any portion could be purchased, be it a head and neck, or a leg, or a gizzard, or a fat entrail; or one could get a live rabbit, a scrawny bristleless pig, a guinea hen, a pigeon or a cooing dove. After visiting the market the party understood how the soup at the hotel came to have so many pieces of chicken neck in it. Up to that time it had seemed as if the birds must have been all neck to furnish sections for all classes of soup, and show so few pieces of the other parts of the frame. The piles of immense yams and sweet potatoes were very attractive in appearance, and equally as fine when tested. Cartloads and pony loads of solid juicy and sweet oranges abounded everywhere, besides luscious pineapples, green or red, the "sapote," "mamey Colorado," and a small fruit resembling in shape and alligator-spotted rind, the pineapple. Roger inquired of a dealer "Como se llama de esta cosa?" to which he instantly replied "anon," and presented him with one. It was a sickly sweet fruit containing many black shiny seeds covered with a soft white pulp. Plantains and bananas were some of them a foot in length. Beets, cabbages, lettuce, radishes, potatoes, etc., differed nothing from home products. Of berries there were none.

The old Tacon market, now known as the "Plaza de Vapores," found only after their drivers had taken them to the "Plaza de Armas" and the fish market, and who wanted pay for each, was the largest, and contained a second story, the latter mostly devoted to poultry and small live animals—including parrots, cockatoos, doves, ducks, goats, pigs, rabbits, etc. The sellers included representatives of all the lower classes—countrymen and negresses. The buyers were often servants, whose baskets would be filled with perhaps a live chicken or a lobster at the bottom, some chicken necks filling in the cracks; a couple slices of fish, a bunch of carrots, a piece of fresh meat, with radishes and lettuce over all, completing the basket, and with the chicken sticking its head up through the center, and cheerfully chirping at exchanging the odoriferous market for the quiet of the dinner table. At the "Plaza de Vapores" the party supplied themselves with gourds at fifteen cents each, after refusing to pay the forty first demanded. Two or three times the men went to the fish market on Empedrado street, but each time it seemed to have been closed for the day, so one morning Roger went around at six o'clock, with a similar result. Then he inquired, and learned that business there only began at one o'clock in the afternoon, and the next time, it was found in operation, on a small scale.

The whole party honored the Sonore restaurant or Café with repeated visits. Its large marble-floored room was filled with tables, mirrors and men, amongst whom an occasional bull fighter swaggered with a long cigar between his lips. The hum and clatter of conversation between a couple hundred customers and loungers, the taps of their jaunty canes on the marble floor, the clapping of hands to signal a waiter, the clouds of smoke from cigars and cigarettes, the music of the band across the Prado in the Isabella park, and the jambs of brokers and loafers at the Tacon theatre entrance across the street in the other direction, all created a strikingly animated scene. This café was where it was said the last Cuban revolution started by the arguments and loud talking of the guests, leading to excitement, and cheers, and crowds, and followed by new hopes, sudden resolves, riot, revolution, and Death. The ices at the Louvre were served with long straws such as Northern boys strove to apply to the bungholes of their fathers' cider barrels. They were also accompanied by thin pastry rolled into cigar-shape. Here, too, they made the acquaintance of a beverage known as a "panale," consisting of a glass of water in which one or two sticks of egg and sugar were dissolved, and producing an excellent drink for babies and dudes. At this place the decanters were first filled with water and then frozen, after which each table was supplied with "a copy." When the fresh water covering the ice in the decanter was exhausted the latter was refilled and refrozen.

Dinero.

The stranger in Cuba was naturally puzzled for a while in receiving and paying money. There was an immense amount of paper afloat issued by "The Spanish Bank of Havana," (whose legal name was said to be "The Spanish Bank of Cuba"). This paper was even dollars and fractional parts thereof, and was kept afloat as long as possible, there being neither redemption nor substitution. He who possessed a piece worn so as to be uncurrent, had to lose it, but the travelers saw none that had reached that point; though to have lost a quarter from one end, on its four corners, or be divided in the middle, or the printing obliterated, was common. Paper was worth 240 per cent less than Spanish gold, and at first the use of such a depreciated currency had a tendency to make an American careless in its use. Roger sending out ten silver dollars for change received twenty-four dollars and seventy-five cents in paper, and the knowledge that he had to spend two dollars and a half before getting rid of a dollar, was demoralizing to economy. Notwithstanding the depreciation of paper, Spanish gold was still worth less than American greenbacks or exchange on New York. In selling New York drafts drawn by the Union Bank of Denver for $250.00, they received $270.00 in newly coined Spanish gold. In buying some dominoes for the ladies the price of $3.50 in gold was reduced to $3.25 when paid in greenbacks. In paying a silver dollar for three lemonades one night during a call from Dr. Wilson, Roger got back seventy cents in subsidiary silver, with none larger than a ten, and most of them five-cent pieces. Every one was punched, which in the smaller pieces had removed about one-tenth of the value. Hence Spanish silver, while superior to paper, was far less preferable than American coin. The computation of values was for a period troublesome, as their silver included such amounts as 6 1/4 cents, 12 1/2 cents, and so forth; while their gold began at $1.06 1/4, and ran along through $2.12 1/2, $4.25, $8.50 and so on. The different values of gold, silver, paper, and greenbacks made it quite necessary to be supplied with plenty of gold and paper, so as not to be obliged to pay in more than one kind at a time. The reverse would occasion more figuring than would be compatible with honest returns in Cuba, unless the purchaser was familiar with the Spanish tongue. For instance, were one to purchase goods amounting to ten dollars in paper it would be inconvenient to offer a gold coin with $1.06 1/4, or $2.55 1/2 in paper, and a two dollar greenback, worth about $5.20; and a silver dollar worth about $2.40, for he would never hear of the fifteen cents change he ought to receive. The best method was found to have plenty of Spanish gold and paper, and pay in that in which the price was quoted, which was sometimes gold and sometimes paper, according to the habit of the particular store. The metal money, besides being punched, was a hospital-looking lot, even to the new gold. The silver was worn smooth and the edges thin. The new gold was thin and lacked those strong lines giving a positive individuality to distinguish American gold and silver. Possibly Americans should not sneer at the Cuban paper money, as their own currency was at as low an ebb less than twenty-five years ago; but the American money depreciated during a war, the result of which none could foresee; and at its close the paper gradually appreciated. In Cuba there was no war, yet the paper did not appreciate. The apparent dishonesty of the government bank, as illustrated in the non-redemption of worn bills, contributed to the general demoralization of financial matters; while a current belief that a smash would occur soon added to the general shakiness.

The notes from five dollars up were nearly twice the size of American National Bank notes, and the fractional currency was similar to that of American war memory—all the work of American engravers. The large double-sized bills had white backs, with no printing, but the backs of the smaller were in green. The paper of all was of inferior quality rapidly wearing at the folds, perhaps selected so as to ensure its more speedy dissolution. New fractional currency was sometimes obtained in long strips and sections torn off as needed. All the aged American jokes about carrying money in a market basket applied with full force in Cuba.

At the bull fight two pedlars were noticed—one carrying his currency in the crown of his hat, which was well filled, and another inside the bosom of his shirt, and which was stuffed with at least two or three quarts of the literally "filthy lucre." Prices depended upon how much the purchaser knew. Several minor conditions entered into the case, but knowledge was the principal ingredient. As a rule they were not very far from Denver prices. Carriage hire was a notable exception. Two passengers could ride to any part of the city within the old walls for forty cents in paper, which was only sixteen cents in American money; and this price, regulated by the authorities, was doubtless the cause of so large a number of carriages being supported in Havana, for all classes being able to ride, did so, even to Negroes and Chinamen. Washerwomen returning a bundle of clothes frequently took a Victoria in preference the narrow and crowded walks. There is food for reflection in this for United States railroad managers.

For future reference the historian adds the amounts paid for various articles and upon diverse trips: oranges unselected, one cent, paper; selected, two cents; bullfight box $20 paper; admission $4.00 each. Tacon theatre box, $20.00 paper; admission $5.00 each; Victoria to Henry Clay cigar factory outside the city limits, $4.00 paper; the "Rosarita" on the bay an hour and a half, with five passengers, $3.00 paper; armless iron chairs at the parque, 10 cents; with arms, 20 cents; at the Louvre two gin cocktails, two lemon ices and one strawberry cream, $2.20 paper; the priest at the Cathedral, $2.00 paper; ferry boat 10 cents paper; street cars 10 to 20 cents; stereoscopic views $1.00; Victoria at Guanabacoa one hour, for five persons, $3.00; bouquet of roses 50 cents; trip to Marianao $4.10 paper; admission to the cockpit, and front seats, $5.00 paper; cigars, similar to $5.50 domestic manufacture, in Denver, $5.00 gold, at the Henry Clay depot; telegrams to Denver $5.40 and $7.80 gold, or 60 cents a word, date and addresses included. According to Rendon milk cost wholesale about 11 cents a quart, and it, by the way, was immediately boiled and salted to keep it fresh; expenses Havana to Matanzas return 2 1/2 persons $18.75 gold; volante to the cave $5.00 gold; to the chapel of Monserrat, $4.00; to the coffee plantation $6.00.

Owing to the inconvenience of language the ladies did but little shopping, but beginning to languish under it, Mike got them ready one day for a trip with Rendon. The latter, however, skipped out, and Mike had to go himself. He returned claiming that he could make none of the storekeepers understand, and therefore nothing had been purchased. The proverb of "Where ignorance is bliss, 'tis folly to be wise," was again proven in this case, for he saved all but his medio peso for carriage hire. Roger went shopping with Anna, and unfortunately took her to a store where they talked in alleged English, so that no money was saved as on the preceding occasion. Among other goods obtained on this occasion was a large stock of pineapple fibre handkerchiefs, made in Barcelona, at 40 cents each in gold; but by her seductive arts on the clerk she succeeded in getting away without paying for some ten or twelve specimens of pineapple dress goods, to see if they would "wash," so that she had enough for her friends as well as a large tract of patch work. After their ride with Rendon one evening they walked through Obispo street, and finally wound up at a fan store, where the dudes behind the counter employed all their arts to sell them souvenir fans, with paintings in gaudy colors of handsome bullfighting cavaliers, but the prices appalled them and they finally left with a promise from Roger, whose underpinning had just about given out, that they would return and buy before leaving town. It was not his fault that they failed to make his promise good. Mike and Roger hunted the town over for stereoscopic views, but only obtained a very few inferior pictures at a dollar each, or six for five dollars. The ladies were also shopping one day with Mrs. Warner, and who advised them to take in their watch chains if they did not want them stolen. On Anna's return she reported that she had bought goods to the amount of $2.45; paid the driver in silver; had changed a $5.30 gold piece, and had only a dollar remaining. After she and Roger had disputed about it for a reasonable length of time she admitted that the balance was in her pocketbook.

LA

Habana Elegante

Semanario dedicado al bello sexo

ÓRGANO OFICIAL DEL CÍRCULO HABANERO.

Director: Ignacio Sarachaga.

SUPLEMENTO.

REDACCION Y ADMINISTRACION: HABANA 90.

HABANA
IMPRENTA EL FENIX, O-REILLY 12.
1886.

CIRCULO HABANERO.

Programa de la velada que tendrá efecto la noche del 25 de Enero de 1886, en el teatro «Irijoa».

Primera parte.

1º { a—Intermezzo
b—Vals lento
c—Spiccato } del Ballet de Silvia, Leo Delibes

Arreglo para doble cuarteto y piano del laureado pianista Ignacio Cervantes, ejecutado por los profesores de la «Sociedad de Conciertos».

2º Vals de la ópera *Dinorah*, cantada por la Srta. Clementina De Vere, artista unánimemente aplaudida en nuestro gran teatro, y que generosamente se ha prestado á tomar parte en esta velada.

3º Epílogo en la ópera *Mefistófele*, del Maestro Boito, cantada por el distinguido tenor cubano Sr. Massanet.

4º *El Poeta y la Golondrina* diálogo en verso recitado por la Srta. Elvira Lopez y el Sr. Gumersindo Lastra.

5º Mosaico de la ópera *Los Hugonotes*, Meyerbeer, ejecutado por el septimino.

6º Aria de tenor en la ópera *La Hebrea* cantada por el Sr. Massanet.

Segunda parte.

La partida de ajedrez: comedia en un acto por la Seccion de Declamacion.

Tercera parte.

Este cuarto se alquila: juguete cómico en un acto, por la Seccion de Declamacion.

PAVONI Y CAJIGAS,
SASTRES, AGUIAR NUMERO 84.

NOTICIAS.

La gran novedad del día, la que sirve de tema á todas las conversaciones, es la proximidad del miércoles (pasado mañana) en cuya noche se efectuará el gran baile anunciado en casa del Sr. D. José Benito Sotolongo, Vocal del *Círculo Habanero.*

Ya se han repartido las invitaciones entre las mejores familias habaneras, las cuales (no lo dudamos) han de salir complacidísimas de la amabilidad y esplendidez del Sr. Sotolongo y su apreciable familia.

El baile será de etiqueta. Tocará la mejor orquesta de la Habana.

***

Ya ha terminado su compromiso la compañía de ópera italiana, á la que sucederá la *troupe* de Mme. Judic.

Lo que mejor han hecho los italianos es *IRSE ....ida.*

***

La mayor parte de los jóvenes elegantes que que concurren á las veladas del *Círculo Habanero,* se visten en casa de **Pavoni y Cajigas,** Aguiar 84.

Pavoni ha cortado más de treinta y siete *fracs* para el baile del Sr. D. José Benito Sotolongo.

***

Pronto se organizará el «Club de Patinadores de la Habana».

Se ha elegido Presidente al Sr. D. Lino Martinez.

***

Transcribimos el programa del baile que ha de efectuarse el miércoles en casa del Sr. de Sotolongo.

Primera parte: Rigodón—Danza—Wals Strauss—Lanceros—Danza—Mazurka—Cuadrilla—Danza.

Segunda parte: Cuadrilla—Danza—Polka—Wals Strauss—Lanceros—Danza—Wals del País—Danza.

Esta casa solo fué fundada para llenar un vacío que se notaba á elegante no dejaba servir. No hay más que visitarla para tener una idea de lo conocido de nuestra casa. Al lado se encuentra bonito, barato y elegante.

LA VILLA DE PARIS está situada en el punto más simpático de la Habana, calle del Obispo 76, al lado de los bosques de Bolonia, y frente á «La Sirena de las Flores» salvés, en el punto que los franceses llamarían Boulevard del Italianos, los madrileños Carrera de San Jerónimo y los americanos el Broadway habanero.

La Villa de París.

LA COMPLACIENTE.
100, Habana 100.

Esta casa, única en su clase, acaba de recibir de París y Viena un elegante y variado surtido de abanicos de granadina con pinturas de alta novedad y de extraordinario mérito.

En abanicos de formas caprichosas y propios para regalos, también hemos recibido una bonita colección, que sale de las formas corrientes.

Hay un colosal surtido de guantes de seda, suecia y cabritilla, de todos tamaños y medidas.

100, HABANA 100.

THEATRES, CLUBS AND MUSIC.

PLAZA DE ARMAS—GOVERNOR'S PALACE.

One of the first movements after reaching Havana was to secure tickets to the Tacon theatre. The front of this edifice was not imposing, but the inside was large enough for a bull ring. Of this theatre it was said: that it was constructed by a once-celebrated smuggler named Captain Marti, for whose capture Captain General Tacon offered a large reward; that Marti by stratagem succeeded in passing the guards at night and securing an audience alone with Tacon in the Governor's Palace in the Plaza de Armas and subsequently exposed the retreats of his confederates, but instead of claiming the offered reward asked for the exclusive privilege of fishing on the coast, which the Captain General granted, on condition that he erect an immense market, that after a time should revert to the government. The ex-smuggler having obtained great wealth by this monopoly, sought another in the theatrical line, which was also granted on condition that he should erect one of the largest and best appointed theatres in the world, and call it the "Tacon" theatre. The place would comfortably seat over 3,000 persons, and contained five rows of boxes and chairs besides the parquette. Three of the rows were boxes, or more appropriately stalls, over the dividing partitions of which the seated occupants could gaze at any part of the house. Though there were more than 2,000 persons in the audience, no young couples were distinguishable unless accompanied by their elders. The ladies were bonneted or bareheaded, and all deeply powdered. Between the acts the gentlemen put on their plug hats and nearly all retired, or made calls upon their lady friends in the boxes. The several rows of boxes were surrounded by partitions of slats like window blinds, and outside these partitions were promenades, where many went to smoke. Those buying entrance tickets without seats also walked here and smoked, or look through the slats at the play, and over the heads of the occupants of the boxes. Just outside the building was a paved court open to the sky, where others strolled and sat and smoked and drank between the acts. The opera was by an Italian company of sixty ladies and gentlemen and two horses, and the audience indulged in clapping, hissing and stamping—the latter two being supposed to indicate disapproval, and which appeared to be a common thing in Cuban theatres. The box ticket was collected from the party during the third act, and shortly afterwards they retired. There were some hundreds of men lining the long vestibule leading to the street, apparently for the purpose of staring at the ladies as they passed out.

The Cervantes variety theatre was occupied by a noisy crowd of men and boys, but no ladies. Most of them were smoking and kept their heads covered. The theatre was small, plain, and full of fleas. The first hour was devoted to a light play, the leading lady in which was a combination of languishing loveliness and tropical devilishness. This was followed by a dance in which stockings and tights were the principal features. At nine o'clock the audience retired, and as soon as the stairway was cleared of the descending crowd a new one rushed up, having already secured tickets of the sidewalk brokers.

By invitation of S.M. Simpson they attended a musical entertainment by the "Havana Club" at the "Teatro Irijia," the grounds of which were enclosed with a high iron fence, and within which were numerous refreshment tables, and gas lamps, making a pretty scene. The handsome theatre was filled with invited guests in fashionable attire—their appearance contrasting favorably with a first-class American audience. Some of the ladies could reasonably claim good looks, and all kept up a constant chatter, broken at intervals by touching up their faces from their powder boxes. This charming practice was so attractive to the Denver ladies that a couple of pocket boxes were secured at the earliest opportunity thereafter. At the end of each number on the program the participants were generously encored, and upon their return, the President, who occupied a box near the stage, presented them with baskets of flowers or jewel boxes. During the entertainment an alarm of fire occurred, a rare thing in a city like Havana, and the flames being visible, nearly created a stampede. Having partaken of all the intellectual pabulum required, the party adjourned to the grounds outside to see what could be done for the physical senses. Anna partook of panales, Jane and Roger adhered to their ices, and Mike took anything that was "filling."

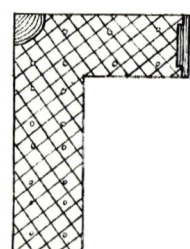

In company with Rendon, who claimed to be a member, the party visited the quarters of the "Casino," or Spanish Club. These were very elegant and extensive, in the form of an L inverted. The marble stairs and floors, massive plate mirrors, beautiful card tables, elegant columns, rare paintings, tasteful stage and band stand, as well as the politeness of the members, was impressive. The gentlemen sitting at the tables conversing or playing, respectfully rose and bowed as the party passed. Among the paintings was one of the Queen by Murillo, and a life size of Cervantes. Both the Casino and Havana clubs have large memberships, and the expenses are very heavy.

On several occasions they visited the parque Isabel to listen to the music of the band, which consisting of many instruments was considered by the natives to be remarkably fine. They found the music lacking in spirit, long and tiresome. Hundreds of people strolled beneath the gas jets or occupied the iron chairs scattered along the walks. Ten cents was charged for an armless chair, and twenty for one with arms, the money being collected by wandering attendants and who gave checks in proof of payment and the right of occupation.

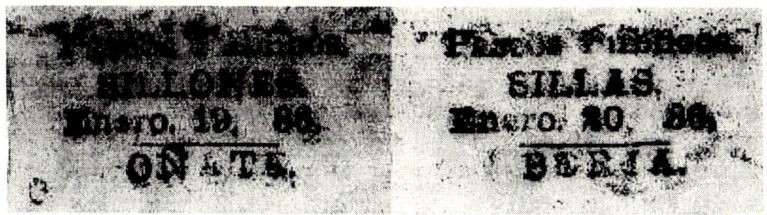

One evening after buying it occurred to Roger to inquire if his check was good for any other chair than that he was occupying, and felt quite elated when he succeeded in making himself understood and received an affirmative reply. Beggars never allowed the stranger many minutes of rest in those chairs. It seemed to be a principle with them that if a person was able to pay for a chair he was able to help a beggar too. One old woman insisted on her mute appeals for aid for several minutes, but only succeeded in getting a number of grunts from the men, and some ohs and ahs from the ladies. The statue of Isabella which adorned the principal park, gave it also its name. As remarking the loyalty of the Cuban to the home government, it was related that at Isabella's dethronement her statue was taken down and imprisoned; but at a subsequent period it was re-erected. The parks were less frequented than in former years, probably because the people possessed less money, and therefore kept fewer private carriages in which the ladies could make a dash. Apparently they cared more for the latter than for the music. The best music heard at Havana was one evening upon the bay, succeeding negotiations in Spanish by Mike and Roger with the swarthy boatmen who navigated the "Rosarita," and who took the two couples and Cook for ninety minutes' ride amongst the steamers and sailing vessels at anchor; and when by the light of the moon their silver and brass voices echoed over the calm waters and hushed the entranced hearers into silence, while the two hardened boatmen, unused from childhood to a stirring of the affections, leaned over the gunwale that their tears might flow unreservedly and unseen into the briny deep. One of the ladies was a trifle frightened upon first leaving the pier, but the music and the amazement combined dispelled all fear. Yet, after the ride, another visit to the park to listen to the big band, and incidentally a call at the Louvre for ice cream, was necessary to restore perfect equilibrium.

The Churches.

How many churches were in Havana the historian did not learn, but he thought not more than in Denver. Not so the priests, however, for on two occasions were seen processions of at least a hundred of them—one just landing of an evening from the "Guanabacoa"; and the other on a Sunday afternoon marching in the neighborhood of La Punta and the royal prison. Individual members of the cloth were seldom observed upon the streets. Those that did appear were well-shaven, their jolly fat cheeks showing unmistakable evidences of their being well fed and securing the best within reach, be it of the "world, the flesh, or the devil." Their sanctification was of the kind so gracefully worn by Friar Tuck in the merry days of Robin Hood in Sherwood Forest; and if Mrs. Warner's declaration was true, the sanctification of the nuns was on a par with that of the clergy. She said that none ever assumed the veil until the last possibility of marriage had gone glimmering. The church edifices were all aged and gray and mossy—none new for many and many a year. Their towers consisted of numbers of arches, each for a bell, and all of which were rung with regard for nothing but noise. The voices of the bells, instead of being brisk and cheerful, were as aged and cracked as everything else in Havana, reviving memories of the old fashioned country bells of childhood days, only the Havana bells sounded so much older—hundreds of years older. They were fittingly allied to the must and dust and rust of the buildings, and seemed to be sounding a requiem for the lost Past and the personal records of the early discoverers and adventurers which have come down to us burnished with the sunset hues of their departed days.

The principal church edifice was the Cathedral, and on the first morning while the men were strolling along Oficios street, they came to an immense ancient edifice that they at once recognized as it, for 300 years at least had rolled over its head, and it was assuredly a church, for the gated doorway was filled with the dirt of years. Later, they pointed out the place to the ladies as once having been the resting place of Columbus, but subsequently they learned that they had made a mistake, and the old church had long belonged to the customs department of the government. On Sunday morning, January 24, after a half hour on the balcony watching the gay scenes in the harbor, and the Spanish flag flying from all the native vessels, as was a Sunday custom, they took Victorias to the real Cathedral, accompanied by Rendon. They entered a passage at the right, and winding around through a number of small courts entered a back door. A young priest in slovenly slipshod garments, unshaven, smoking the last year's stump of a black cigar, received and conducted them up a flight of ten or twelve narrow and steep stone steps to a place where the priests sat when assembled in church service. In the center was a revolving pedestal, with music books twenty inches square, the notes and music being printed large enough to be visible from the priests' seats twelve feet distant. On the wall at the left was a religious picture about a foot square which the priest said was brought over by Columbus, and which the Americans mentally doubted because the Madonna was an Indian. Opposite was a marble slab in the wall with a bust in relief of Columbus, and beneath which was the following inscription:

"Oh! restos é imagen del grande Colon,
Mil siglos durad guardados en la urna
Y en la rebembranza de nuestra nacion."

The most approved translation of this heavy triplet was as follows:

"Oh! remains and image of the great Columbus:
A thousand ages endure preserved in this urn,
And in the remembrance of our nation."

This was rather affecting when it was remembered that Columbus was an Italian, and after the King and Queen had granted him a perpetual commission as Governor of the lands he might discover, he was superseded and sent home in chains. There were quite a number of altars along the sides and old paintings on the walls, while the arched ceiling was frescoed in a light-greenish blue with brown veins. The general shape of the inside will appear from the subjoined diagram.

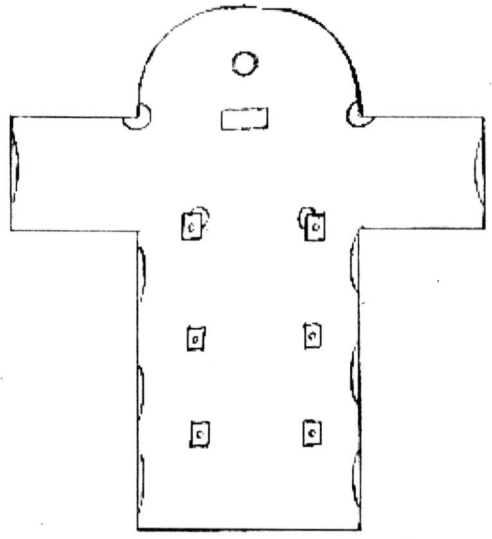

In the robing room adjoining one of the wings were some twenty drawers, of large size, containing the vestments of the church dignitaries richly embroidered with gold and silver bullion, and adorned with diamonds, rubies, emeralds, opals, topaz, etc. There were also closets for hanging robes, and gold and silver service, candlesticks, etc., in great number, estimated at 500 pounds in weight. In a cabinet, the sides and front of which swung back on hinges so as to fully expose its con- tents, was a gold and silver tower in elegantly wrought design like an im- mense monument, said to be worth $25,000, and which could not have been overrated. It was about four feet square at the bot- tom, and eleven or twelve in height, and beneath the

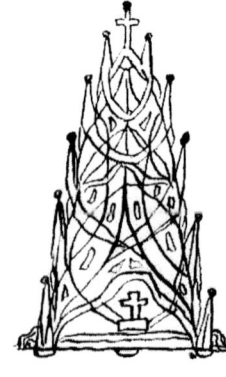

main arch was a golden cross a foot long, in which was set rubies as large as marbles, besides large diamonds and emeralds. A long white robe like a nightgown was done up in an exquisite manner, crimped in quarter-inch folds of irregular direction but joining with nice exactness. The slipshod young father declared the entire value of the property gathered within the bosom of that church to be a million dollars, but it was already past "ten o'clock" and the Americans mentally divided by two, and subtracted one-half. After completing the inspection Slipshod received a two-dollar bill with as much avidity as the naturalized American citizen at a primary election, and then the party proceeded to the auditorium to witness the "service." Fifty or sixty women and a few men attended, shaded all the way to pure ebony, most of them kneeling upon the marble floor throughout the service. At one part, all that were standing dropped to their knees but Mike and Roger, at which several men looked as if an outrage had been committed. The señoras wore black veils, and all, negroes included, briskly plied their fans as they knelt. A servant or slave, accompanying her mistress, knelt behind the latter and duplicated all her crosses and signs. The dresses of the ladies were of cheap simple materials, but cool and spring-like. The service was conducted by one priest and a boy at an altar in one of the wings. The gamin wore a very dirty white shirt or robe over his dirtier clothing, and was kept moderately busy seizing the tail of the Priest's regalia when the latter knelt; and tinkling a bell when he dropped on one knee nearly to the floor, and then bobbed serenely up again without having touched bottom. The Priest made many "passes" at the crucifix in his front, and closed by eating a wafer and drinking some wine. The golden wine cup he tipped high, but the wafer he seemed to care but little for. The bells of the two towers jingled occasionally during service, and the worshipers frequently crossed themselves and made various motions on face and breast that were quite indistinguishable in detail to the uninitiated. If evidence was necessary to disprove the Cuban claim that the body of the devout Columbus was still deposited in the Cathedral, it would be furnished by the absence of kicking in his tomb at the shallow mummery practiced in the name of Heaven in such close proximity.

All the churches that were visited possessed the same general appearance—a few kneeling women, a number of large burning tapers, and a priest in front of one of the altars made picturesque and beautiful with carved figures of the holy personages. The priest was always, during service hour, going through the Latin exercises with his back to his meagre audience, indulging in numerous crosses and other motions indistinguishable in detail to the Protestant. But he was never so deeply engrossed that he could not look around to see the American party enter, and take a hasty survey of their appearance.

Fronting the Captain General's palace in the Plaza de Armas stood a little chapel in the yard of which was a monument marking the site of a tree which stood there when the place was selected for a city, and beneath the branches of which the first mass was said. This little chapel was only opened to the public once a year, on St. Christopher's Day.

On church or feast days, one or two of which occurred during their visit, many persons took holidays, and less business was transacted than usual—about the same as on Sundays.

The nuns of Havana were not often observed on Sunday or any other day in public. Their worldly sisters appeared to entertain a not very exalted opinion of their religious convictions, declaring that none ever assumed the veil until the last vestige of hope of marriage had taken wings and flown away.

The party never wondered at the low tone of morals in Cuba, and they could not but believe the Church responsible for it. It was said that during Lenten season a notice like the following was always made public: "... His Extremely Illustrious Excellency, Señor Bishop Diocesan, makes known to all and each one of the faithful that goes to hear the word of God in this holy season, that he concedes to them forty days of indulgence for each time that they thus do so; and also, as special apostolic favor, a full indulgence to those that attend four sermons in said missions, and confess and worship devoutly," etc. It was the opinion of the party that the island needed the infusion of a religion which would teach people to think and reason on religious and moral matters for themselves, and not leave it exclusively to the priests; and that the missionary societies of America could do no better work in Asia than in Cuba.

THE FORTS.

The first objects to attract attention on approaching Havana are the forts, and they also give the last view to the fleeing stranger. The muzzles of their guns pointed everywhere except into the sky, and the Spanish soldier was a regular luxury at public buildings and on the streets. Visitors were usually admitted to the forts, but passes were first essential from the commanding officers or higher authority. This party, or sections of it, had no hesitation in attempting to pass wherever there were guards, but were always stopped if without a pass. Once Mike and Roger began to walk across a small plaza where cannon were stored, and the guard on the further side at once waved them back; but they would not understand it, and kept on until his musket barred further advance. Then they explained that they only wanted to know if there was any objection to their going up the street nearby, and along which people were constantly passing. They failed to exactly understand what the guard replied, but just turned and walked away as if it was all right. They also sought to enter the Punta, but the guards laughed and shook their heads when they were a hundred feet away. The Punta was begun like Morro in 1589, and was at the right hand of the entrance to the harbor on a low point of land, as its name indicated.

La Fuerza, near the Captain General's palace, was the oldest, being begun by order of Governor Hernando de Soto in 1528. Here it was that the Governor's wife died, after vainly waiting many years for his return from his great expedition to the Continent, which resulted in the discovery of Florida and the Mississippi River, and De Soto's final death, and burial in a log on the edge of the great stream. Mike and Roger entered the grounds and buildings but were neither molested nor questioned.

Anna and Roger visited "Castillo del Principe" on a hill near the western border of Havana, from which a beautiful view of city, country, and ocean was obtained. They entered the parade ground by consent of the guard, over a clumsy drawbridge operated by iron chains and a windlass, from inside the sallyport, and the raising of which covered the latter like a shield. Strolling slowly across the parade ground the officer of the guard requested a pass, by figuratively writing on the palm of his hand with his finger. Roger shook his head, which was then repeated by the officer with a shrug of the shoulders, as much as to say that he was sorry, but he had no discretion, was only obeying orders himself, and was obliged to refuse admission. But as they were already in the center of the fort, they saw all that a pass would have permitted, and slowly retired, completing their examination on the way.

One morning before breakfast Mike and Roger walked to the arsenal further up the harbor, and to which they were admitted by the Sergeant of the guard, who sent a young soldier as escort. The broad walks, flowerbeds and grounds were well kept, but with the exception of a large machine shop stocked with heavy machinery, there was nothing of particular interest. Having become accustomed to giving fees for services a small one was tendered the young soldier, but which he declined, and they parted company at the gates with a lift of the hat and "muchos gracios."

The thick walls and high altitude of the forts gave them an appearance of impregnability, but modern guns of heavy calibre would send their missiles through and through them, and soon tumble the walls down the high bluffs on which they stood.

The most extensive fortification was the Cabañas, which was in full view from the San Carlos across the bay, and was visited by the party on the 22^d of January. Alighting from their victorias at Quay Caballeria they embarked in "Dos Amigos" 245, and were in five minutes on the opposite shore. There they found a gentle ascending avenue paved with cobblestones set in lime, which after several sharp turns, being in all probably 1000 feet in length, led to the entrance, which was a lane or avenue between two sections of the fort. The walls were smoothly plastered with cement, once painted yellow, and were probably fifty feet high. The avenue was about the same width also, and in the center was a row of handsome Indian laurel trees, the tops of which covered the entire width, and formed a beautiful cool and shady plaza for some 300 feet. After passing a sentry there they twisted around from one avenue or court to another, and through an open arch to the headquarters of the officers of the day and guard,—a long, low, cool, arched room, where they waited while Rendon spent a half hour interviewing the commanding officer for a pass. Then skirting the long guard-house or prison, through the grated windows of which numerous culprits were seen, they wound into the parade ground, and look out across the harbor to the city, the ocean, and the country, even to the Pau mountains of Matanzas, sixty miles distant. The fort was armed with long old-fashioned bronze or brass pieces of light calibre, bearing pet names, and figures—the latter being

either the year of manufacture in the last century, or the number of a "job lot," averaging below first-class. They had evidently not been rubbed up for some years, and were green with dampness and time. The shot were piled in conical heaps and plastered with lime for protection from the elements, and few of the monuments still perfect, while from others the lime had crumbled, leaving the balls exposed, and honeycombed and eaten with rust. By a wide inclined plane they ascended to the top of the casemates, and for a half-hour wandered around its 800 yards of length, but at the end with no very precise idea of

its complicated form. Here they lingered to examine a long gun; there at one of the angles, squeezed into a little old watch tower to peer through its narrow slits; again climbing the two high steps to survey from the parapet the ocean on the moat; descending steep crumbled steps at one point, and ascending at another, until finally they departed at the end next to Morro, and walked by a countryfied road to the latter, the entrance to which was up another long paved avenue, of less extent than that leading to the Cabañas. The entrance to this celebrated fort was there an arch, within which were benches and upon which a number of soldiers were lounging, but who politely vacated them for the ladies while Rendon sought the commandant for permission to enter the castle. At one side of the arch was a barred prison door, and through the grating protruded a long nose, which they were told was attached to a newspaper man who had said something objectionable to the Captain General, and for which he was given a two-years vacation in Morro. One of the ladies having a liking for newspaper men gave him a flower through the bars, which caused him to express his grateful thanks and dream of the girl he left behind him. Far beneath the outer prison, and beyond the reach of interrogating visitors, were said to be extensive dungeons, where for more than 300 years personal spite and suspicion had consigned men to darkness, despair, death, decay and oblivion. Like the mouth of Hell, he who entered there left all hope behind. Morro was smaller than the Cabañas, but in better repair. Its walls were high above the sea, and when looking down upon the moat from the top of the casemates the distance appeared to be seventy-five feet. To this it was arranged to admit the sea, thus completely surrounding the castle with water. The guns were newer than those of Las Cabañas, and evidently of American manufacture. After making themselves all too weary for persons bent on pleasure, they climbed into the little signal station, upon the numerous shelves of which were laid the flags of all nations, and where they took a drink all 'round from the usual earthen jar with a sandpaper mouth, and looked through the big telescope. When one of the party put his hat over the big end while Mike was trying to see a whale in the distance, Mike began with "Say, Mister, there's something the matter with Hello there you take that hat off or you'll get into trouble."

Last of all they reached the "O'Donnell Lighthouse," and as their eyes climbed upward 78 feet to its airy summit, their hearts hastened downwind 80 feet to the level of the sea. Fuller and Mrs. Hummel declared that they preferred to search for curiosities along the shore, but the others shook out an extra bit of determination and refused to turn back or acknowledge defeat. A knock at the door caused the keys to be flung down from above, the attending guard opened the door, and they slowly toiled up the circular ascent. The 122 marble steps gradually grew narrower and steeper, until finally they were but a trifle superior to a ladder, with the space overhead so cramped that the visitors were obliged to crawl upwards on their bellies. The pure white cut glass Fresnel light consisted of concentric rings with sharp faces, inside of which they also crawled and examined the complicated machinery by means of which a reflector was made to alternate with the regular light for a space of six seconds each half minute. It was a hard climb, especially for the ladies, but though every muscle quivered, and their knees wobbled and doubled beneath them on descending, and the perspiration poured from Mike's roof as if he had eyes all over it and all were weeping, they felt more than repaid; and walking slowly back to the boat they fetched the city in two tacks.

Fortifications of some kind could be found most anywhere on the outskirts of the city—all old, some merely circular towers, and others little bits of parapet with a watch tower here and there with its 2x8 slits through which the sentinel peered for the enemy. The old walls of Havana, traced out in 1589, but not finished until 1724, were nearly obliterated, having survived only about the same length of time as was required for their construction. Small remnants were visible at two or three points in what had become the heart of the city—massive rusty masonry, ten feet high and from four to six thick. Outside of Havana the party saw no forts and few soldiers. The power of Spain seemed to be concentrated mainly at the Capital, and there it was the most needed. If the people grumbled at the expense they could appropriately remember that their sports, immoralities and natural deviltry made the presence of many guards a necessity. He who dances must pay for the fiddler.

THE WEED.

When Columbus dispatched a party of sailors into the interior of Cuba to carry a letter from Ferdinand and Isabella to the Grand Khan of Cathay, whose country he supposed he had reached, they observed on their return some natives smoking a weed rolled in a leaf which they called "a tobaco," and which has since been applied to the weed itself. And where its use was first discovered it had come into universal use; unlike America; however, it was only employed in smoking. Five cents would buy a dozen cigarettes, and the Cuban had at least one pocket devoted to their stowage. Every half hour or so one of these would be re-rolled, a few whiffs taken and exhaled through the nostrils and the stump flung away. Many also employed the ordinary cigar, while others still delighted in a big black club of tobacco at least seven inches in length. Smoking was permitted anywhere unless in church during service, and a lady's parlor or a public table at a hotel were no exception. The habit of smoking between the courses at table may have originated in an effort to discover something to neutralize the taste of Spanish cooking, and if so, was excusable. Americans sometimes sought to wear a Cuban air by pursuing the island custom at table, but with the exception of nephew Fuller this party did not join the number. Cuban women are not wholly exempt from the use of the weed, and on several occasions ladies in fine robes and respectable-appearing dwellings were observed in their everlasting rocking chairs with something more substantial than a cigarette between their lips; but upon the street none of the softer sex except negroes advanced in years were seen to smoke, and then always immense black cigars or their stumps, and with perhaps a great bundle upon the head. With one arm akimbo, they swung along with a lordly stride, as if all the necessities of life were provided in the big cigar, and enjoying "gol-snorting" comfort. Cigarettes were sold almost everywhere except in dry goods and clothing stores, and were manufactured in even more places. The doorkeeper at the entrance of a first-class residence thus employed his spare time, and exhibited some hundreds or thousands of specimens at his elbow. Youth, old age, nor beggary was a bar to the use of tobacco, and very needy looking specimens of humanity were sometimes to be seen on the streets with a cigarette behind each ear for immediate use as an American clerk may carry his pen or pencil. One day while Anna and Roger were riding to La Punta, they passed some young negro men with boxes of seven-inch cigars for which they appeared to have been sent by their masters. Being better goods than they were in the habit of using, the temptation was too much for one, who not daring to abstract a cigar, had opened the box, and was licking with his big tongue the whole top layer thus exposed; while his companions stood looking on and awaiting their turn.

The factories were numerous. Roger bore a letter to proprietor Alvarez of the largest on the island, whose father established the business and died a month previous. At his "Henry Clay" depot at 9 1/2 O'Reilly, they made their purchases—the gold prices by the box being but little below those of an American cigar of similar quality. By invitation of young Alvarez they rode to the factory two or three miles out near Jesus del Monte, and where he met and accompanied them through one of the buildings, of which he had several on both sides of the street. While exhibiting the working of his factory and his great stores of leaf, he had a workman pull a handful from a bale that had received no treatment, and from which a cigar was made for each. It contained all the nicotine and he said

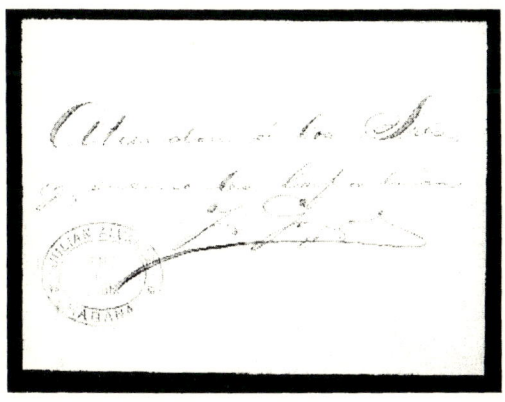

could not be regularly smoked without affecting the heart. It proved to be a delightfully fine smoke, almost void of the taste of tobacco, and the ladies themselves politely declared that its odor was very refreshing and superior to toilet perfumes. They thought they would like a little of it themselves on the sly. Alvarez presented each of the gentlemen with samples of different sizes and qualities, including one wrapped in gold leaf and selling at $500.00 a thousand; also a box of twenty-five just made. He employed 900 hands, and he estimated the expense of the privilege they enjoyed of smoking all they wished, to be $75,000 a year. He suggested that it was quite a tax, but upon intimation that American consumers had to make it up, he ventured an affirmative smile. Señor Alvarez had been in Denver, and the party earnestly besought him to go again and give them an opportunity to reciprocate his courtesies.

THE ROYAL LOTTERY.

The royal lottery was the best-advertised "cosa de Cuba," the drawings of which occurred in the cool of the early hours each alternate Saturday. Hundreds of men and women were hawking the tickets about the streets from early in the morning until late a night—few of them able-bodied in any department except lungs. In that cripples were thus given a means of livelihood, the lottery might be considered a blessing, but then they could as well have sold something else in the same way. As soon as one drawing was finished the tickets for the next were exposed, and as the day of drawing drew near they went off rapidly. A street broker's stock in trade consisted of a crutch, a roll of soiled tickets, and a pair of scissors, the latter to divide a

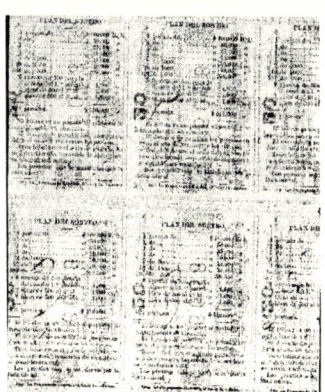

ticket when desired. The day of the party's arrival in Havana immediately preceded the 1206th drawing, and the brokers were shouting "m-a-ñ-a-n-a" as if the last opportunity of becoming a Jaygould by the investment of a few paper dollars was about departing forever. For a couple of weeks the Americans paid no attention to the numerous solicitations which poured in upon them, but then at the request of Mr. Simpson, from whom they had accepted some favors, they joined him in a purchase, and drew a blank. Two weeks later, having become partially demoralized, they again invested in a twentieth of three tickets, excusing themselves on the plea that they had taken their wives into partnership, and desired to do the handsome thing by giving them half of the proceeds. They drew blanks once more, but on each occasion sufficient numbers hovered around each side of their own to inveigle imagination into demanding just one more chance.

"For of all the words of tongue or pen,
The saddest are: It might have been."

Had their Havana sojourn continued they would doubtless soon have become regular contributors to the lottery like the average native. It was a cold day when any of the latter permitted a drawing without having invested. It was considered as one of the essential ingredients of domestic felicity, and as necessary to ensure healthy digestion and sound repose, as plenty of olive oil and garlic. Even the negro with a gunnysack shirt and the beggar on the street would soon have lapsed into disappointed corpses if robbed of their semi-monthly opportunities of acquiring sudden wealth. Beggars and lottery tickets appeared to be closely allied, and occupants of a carriage upon alighting sometimes had the choice of one upon the right and the other on the left.

On the morning of January 30 Roger rose early, from asthma, and went upon the street at half past five. It was scarcely light, but men and boys were already numerous with the fragments of unsold tickets, excitedly shouting the numbers they bore, and that the drawing was to occur that day; as: "Hoy! hoy! cuatro ciento y seis! hoy! hoy!" Mike and Roger hastened down to Lottery Square at nine, but were too late for anything but the crowds scanning the bulletins, and the final checking of the returns. One of the judges was an old man who lived at the San Carlos, and being desirous of witnessing the next drag they arranged through Rendon to accompany him. Accordingly at daylight on the 13th of February they did so, their guide introducing them in Spanish to his associates as Americans, and according them seats with the judges, where everything was before their eyes. All the judges being in place the fun began. A four-foot globe of narrow brass bands was a quarter filled with wooden marbles, upon which numbers had been burned corresponding to each ticket issued. A two-foot globe of similar construction was filled to the depth of six inches with marbles

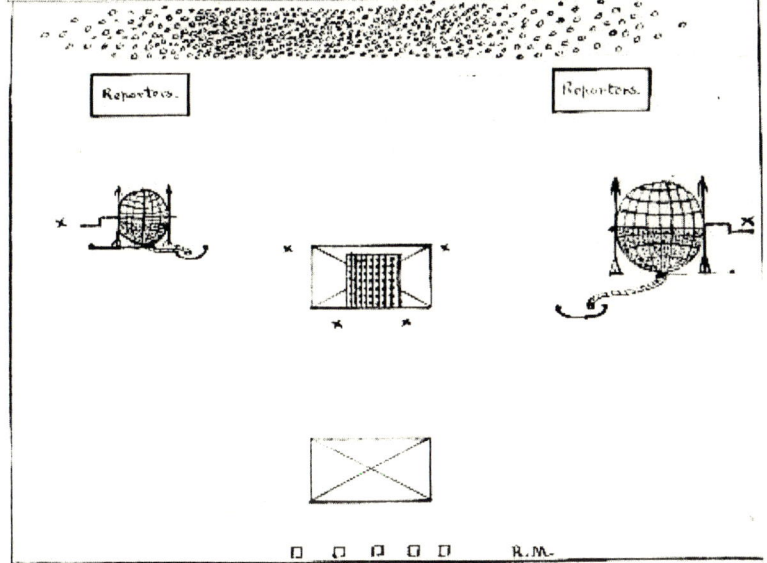

marked with the prizes, from $500 to $100,000. The marbles were visible to the bystanders through the interstices. By an attendant at each globe pulling open a valve a single marble was permitted to escape from each, which rolled along a wire spout in full view, for about five feet, when it was discharged into a glass vessel. Two bright boys of a dozen years picked the marbles from the dishes and holding them before the audience announced the numbers in loud voices—first from the large globe representing the ticket, and then the value of the prize, from the small globe. Upon a center table was a frame containing twenty parallel wires, and upon which the marbles were strung by the boys. Wires for ticket marbles and prize marbles alternated, and when the frame of twenty wires or two hundred prizes, was filled, the ends were locked and another frame employed. Two men sat in front of that table to watch the boys and superintend the wires. As rapidly as the numbers were read by the boys they were bulletined on immense blackboards; and every forty numbers the globes were revolved a few times by means of cranks, thoroughly re-mixing the marbles within. When the last marble fell from the small globe the excitement was over and everyone drew long breaths of relief. The blackboards were then taken before the judges and the number on the marbles carefully re-read by one of them aloud for comparison with the blackboards and the record made by the Secretary. In all sixteen persons were engaged in the drawing, besides a dozen reporters and a couple of hundred men of mixed respectability and various degrees of pecuniary interest. The reporters frequently dispatched copy to their offices by messengers, so that in a few minutes after the finish printed lists of the lucky numbers were purchasable on the street. The official list appeared in the afternoon. So far as the Denver men could perceive the drawing was not only fairly conducted, but there was no practicable method of defrauding. After witnessing the entire proceedings they shook hands with the gray-headed judges and retired with muchos gracios, just in time to run against a stub-legged fellow entering at the gate and shouting out tickets for the next drawing.

THE COCK PIT.

On the last day of January the two men rode to the Inglaterra hotel to accompany Simpson to the "Valle de Gallos," where for some hours each Sunday a couple of hundred men gathered to fight game cocks and bet away their week's wages. The pit was in an out-of-the-way building not far from the Plaza de Toros and the ring was not more than 25 feet in diameter. It was immediately surrounded by a low fence, back of which was a single row of chairs for those who preferred fancy seats. Above and back of this were several other rows of benches. Over the center of the pit was hung a loud bell and some steelyards, and the pit was filled with men, white and black, mostly coatless and vestless, arguing the merits of respective cocks. A pedlar or two circulated amongst the crowd with peanuts and pared oranges. After considerable delay the boss jangled the bell for the entry of the birds, and two or three bags were soon presented, from which, after weighing, the cocks were taken. They were very small, their combs cut close, the neck and back feathers picked out, and the skin treated with liquids so as to have become tough and hard. The men in charge taking the birds in their hands crowd them around the ring to exhibition, during which, Pandemonium reigned. All were yelling and contorting as if their souls depended on winning their neighbor's money. No cash was flaunted, but the bets were rapidly completed, some making notes but most of them trusting to memory. A big negro on the top seats at one side, clinging to a post with one arm, and leaning down over the seats below, shouting and pounding and gesticulating, would be taken up by a white frantic idiot opposite, the bargain made by a snap of the fingers in an instant, and the operation proceeded for another contract without a moment's hesitation. As all were participating in the scramble at the same time, Bedlam was no circumstance to it, and could the old sinners from ancient Babel have looked upon the scene they would have paled with envy and chagrin. Finally the boss rung the bell again and sought to clear the pit, but the people were slow to vacate and it was only by main force that he finally pushed them out. Then the men in charge of the cocks filled their mouths with liquid from a big black bottle and spirted the contents in a fine spray upon the heads, necks, and under the tails of the birds, and after making a pass or two, tossed them gently upon the ground towards each other. Up to that instant the birds had been as quiet and docile as doves, thoroughly accustomed to being handled, and sitting quietly in their keepers' hands; but upon touching the ground and facing one of their kind, their whole nature seemed to change in an instant, and they flew at each other as if an old Southern feud had existed in their families for generations, and was about to be permanently settled. The first fight was a long one, and the weaker cock prolonged his existence a quarter of an hour by running around the ring with his pursuer a few inches in the rear. Round and round they went, the pursuer sometimes gaining a trifle by reducing the circle and making a dash at the other's neck, when for an instant there would be a skirmish at close quarters, and then the race would re-commence. During this scene the actions of the swarthy fellow who had charge of the fleeing cock were ludicrous beyond description. Squatting at the outer edge of the ring, or jumping wildly from side to side, his arms flung out in front, his fingers wide extended and working convulsively, his features undergoing the most wonderful contortions, he kept up a continual yelling like the Devil himself when an honest man treads on the fork of his tail. Mike and Roger were unable to keep their eyes from him, nor their mouths closed, but in sheer astonishment at his wonderful gyrations kept shouting in each other's ear to "Look at that fellow for Heaven's sake!" He was the most demented of the lot, but all who had bet were equally as interested though not spreading it on so thick. The bull ring of Havana, the old gold pit of New York and the wheat pit of Chicago on the blackest of "black Fridays," could not excel the little cock pit of calle de Manrique. Finally the fleeing bird was overtaken by his pursuer and laid low by a spur-thrust in the head. Then the boss held aloft a minute-glass, and when the sand had run out, reversed it, repeating the performance four or five times, and the disabled bird being still incompetent to renew the combat, it was decided in favor of the crowing cock, and the people went around good naturedly to pay their bets. The keeper of the defunct bird suddenly sobered down and never yipped again during the balance of the day. Before the next fight, Mike's curiosity was aroused at the black bottle, and smelling at the nozzle he pronounced it brandy and water; without having to taste it at all. The second fight was of brief duration, a spur-thrust in the head laying one of the contestants out almost at the beginning. His body remained full of fight and his courage good, but he was too dizzy to keep his feet and was obliged to surrender. The victor pecked at his head and eyes so long as they allowed him to lie upon the ground, and then indulged in a valiant crow, like all of those which won. In the fourth fight one of the cocks was owned by a negro, from whose attention the bird seemed to be at least a family relation, or else constituted his entire worldly possessions. No man could fight more persistently to preserve his property from destruction than this fellow did to protect his cock. His was the weaker of the two, and whenever its opponent was getting the upper hand, he would snatch up his own, spirt brandy and water over its head, neck, and rear, suck its wounds, blow into its throat, and ruffle its tail feathers. The crowd became impatient and finally began to laugh at his persistence; and still later broke into loud peals of merriment and derision whenever he dashed for his bird. This made him huffy, and finally he relinquished the contest and carried his bird away for medical treatment and future contests. It showed lameness at the start, and besides, was handicapped by the shortening of its spurs by the use of wax and twine, and probably lost the battle from those causes.

The Denver party witnessed four battles and then pulled out for other Sunday scenes.

PLAZA DE TOROS.

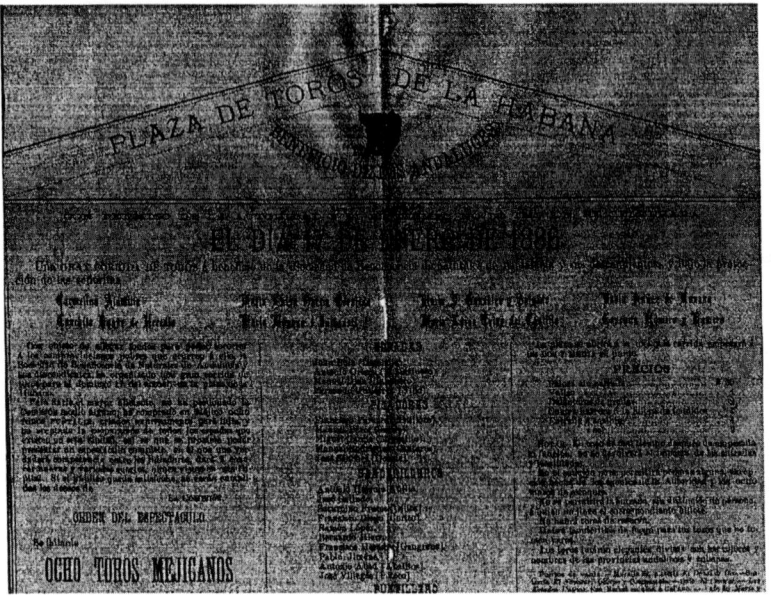

Visitors to a strange land, if at all curious, acquaint themselves with such novel practices as have made the people notorious; and if not curious it is presumed they might as well remain at home. The ladies in this party appeared to think that a visit to a bull fight would imply approval of the sport, or a desire to witness one, and therefore objected to attend; but the gentlemen insisted that they should never return home without the ability to speak intelligently of a national sport of such renown. Admission tickets and a box were accordingly secured for the first Sunday afternoon, when each couple took Victorias for the Plaza de Toros on the opposite side of the city. Evidences of the approaching contest began to appear when they had two miles yet to go—first by a couple of wagons conveying two long poles from which dangled many banderilleros or darts, covered with gay ribbons. A little later when they had passed through the Campo Marte and struck into the Calzada Reina, they noted scores of victorias all proceeding in the same direction as themselves, each occupied by one, two, or three persons, while returning carriages were all vacant. A little further and the calzada became the Paseo Tacon, with few buildings to obstruct the view to the bull ring, still nearly a mile beyond, and the sight of which seemed to stimulate every driver to fury. They lashed their little horses to cut in here or crowd out there, always seeking to pass the vehicle next in front, and hurrying on pell-mell until arriving at a side street upon which the ring was situated. At a fountain in the center of the Paseo Tacon sat a silent cavalryman with a drawn sabre, to preserve order and see that each carriage for the ring passed around the fountain on the outside and fell into line in the street to the left. The quarter of a mile from there on was literally filled with two columns of victorias, one slowly advancing and unloading, and the other hastening back to the city for more passengers. There were certainly many hundreds in all, and Mike thought there were thousands; while Anna excitedly declared there were millions. At intervals between the two lines sat cavalrymen with drawn sabres, whose presence prevented confusion and a blocking of the street by drivers anxious to get in ahead so as to ensure a speedier return. The building containing the ring was an immense grandstand forming a complete circle around a hundred-foot ring. It was painted brick color, was about thirty feet high, and boarded tight. Entering beneath the seats and ascending a short flight of stairs brought the visitor into the grandstand proper, facing the arena, the floor of which was pounded hard and smooth. First around the ring was a five-foot fence, along which about fifteen inches from the ground, ran a "two by four" that served as a step to facilitate leaping. The fence was separated from the front of the grandstand by a six-foot passage. This front was tightly boarded to a height of seven feet, and then ten rows of benches followed for ordinary admissions. Next was a row of boxes or stalls containing four chairs each for ladies and such as chose to pay for them; while still above was a second row of ten benches mostly occupied by armed soldiers. The entire seating capacity was about 10,000. The principal box was for the President of the Association, and beside it another for the Captain General of the

Island. Upon the entrance of the President the crowd yelled and cheered as if he had just donated a large fortune to charity, to which he bowed low many times, and with gracious smiles placed his hand over the spot where his heart should be, and sat down. Then the music struck up, the gates beneath the seats at one side opened, an expert rider on a handsome horse cantered in, saluted the President, and rode once around the ring to the place of entrance. Then placing himself at the head of the professionals he led them on a grand march to the front of the President, whom they saluted, and at once prepared for business. In the procession were about thirty persons, certainly enough to ensure the death of the bulls, one at a time. There were sixteen footmen, five horsemen, eight negro boys, and two three-mule teams. The negroes wore red shirts; the mules were treated a trifle better, their coverings being ornamented with gold and silver borders; but the professional fighters were gorgeously attired in scarlet, yellow, blue, green, and purple, with a profusion of gold and silver trimmings. They were men of fine physique, and some of them wore long hair put up in a knot at the back of the head like a woman.

The mules being driven out, a blast of a bugle signaled the opening of the gate to the dark bull pens immediately opposite where the men entered. Attracted by the light the bull at once entered on the run, and upon crossing the six-foot alley surrounding the fence, a barbed rosette of gaily colored ribbons and spangles was thrust into his back by some one secreted behind the gate which for the time being was shut back across the alley, but which on being again closed made the fence perfect. Different bulls began business in different ways. All had long sharp horns, and a majority instantly assailed the nearest object. Some halted in bewilderment and trotted off in a frightened sidelong way, making a dash now and then, but seeming to do so under protest. The receiving force consisted of two picadores or horsemen, and six or seven banderilleros or footmen, in addition to which a couple of the red-shirted negroes were in attendance upon each horse. The latter having been worn out in the service of man, and being too old for more, were purchased for a few dollars as the cheapest sources of such blood letting as was essential to create an appearance of danger in a bull fight. Their riders generally sat facing the center of the ring, their horses blindfolded in one eye, and made no effort to keep away from a bull. They were armed with long lances with brads at the ends, and which the bull usually avoided after a taste; but the riders never exerted themselves very much, for their legs being wrapped with hide their own danger was trifling, and the goring and ripping of a horse but added to the rider's apparent courage and coolness. The horses themselves, however, were sometimes less indifferent, as was illustrated by one which for an instant revived the fire of youth, when he discovered that his rider could not be depended on to protect him, and delivered two or three severe kicks with both hind feet upon the ribs of an angry bull. The banderilleros had nothing at first but blood-stained cloths, once red on one side and yellow on the other—in size six or eight feet by three or four. They approached near the bull and flinging one end of their banners toward him, started for the fence, trailing the banners behind, the bull pursuing with lowered head. The animal never plunged as represented in pictures, but loped or trotted at a gait that any active man could easily avoid. The banderilleros sealed the fence, however, whenever a bull was nigh, by placing a foot on the two-by-four near the bottom, and a hand upon the top. Sometimes the horns of a bull brought up against the fence, but it never appeared that he was after the man—either in the ring or when taking the fence—but the rag trailing behind him. Barring the strain of seriousness, it was like a child trailing a string and a kitten endeavoring to catch it. If the bull got his horns near the cloth, he tossed his head as if he had captured his enemy, and at the toss, stopped his career. The probability was that after such a toss he would follow that cloth no longer but turn to another. The men therefore appeared quite safe themselves if they kept their feet and flirted their flags aside before the bull was too close upon them. The banderilleros and picadores of course worked harmoniously together. If the bull refused to attack the horses the riders, to preserve their reputations, usually urged their blinded beasts to advance so as to invite a charge. Out of the ten bulls the writer saw slaughtered, only one was prompt to assail the horses, and he seemed to enjoy it. He trotted straight toward them and halting on arrival, threw up his head so as to plunge them their whole length into the horse's breast or shoulder, and then with their blood streaming down into his eyes, slowly lifted them over upon their haunches, the riders in the meantime looking out for their own cowardly legs as their horses went slowly down. One horse was caught by the fence and when lifted up his rider went over the other side into the alley, apparently glad that a stout fence separated him from the bull. The goring of a horse was never the result of a running plunge of the bull's body, but the toss of his powerful neck. During the assault on a horse the banderilleros never failed to make sufficient diversion so as to attract the bull away before finishing his work; still, the three horses gored by this particular bull could hardly regain their feet, and then only by severe pounding, which was continued while they staggered from the ring. By the time a bull had been in the ring five or six minutes he began to realize that there were too many for him, and his aggression oozed away. Then the bugle sounded, the picadores retired, and the banderilleros brought in their barbed darts heretofore spoken of, and the employment of which seemed to be attended with some danger. Taking one in each hand and brandishing them aloft, the banderillero faced the bull fifteen or twenty feet away. Accepting the defiant gestures as a challenge, the bull approached with lowered head to the attack, while the banderillero also advanced by rapid steps only a few inches in length so as to facilitate turning aside without the loss of an atom. A half inch too close at the moment of contact might mean failure for the man and success for the bull. At the instant of meeting the bull halted so as to toss his head to greater advantage and at that moment the banderillero reached his darts forward and plunged them into his neck just forward of the shoulders, or wherever he could reach, and did it so quickly as to avoid the toss of the bull's horns, and then instantly sprang away. The bull shook his head and turned as if to pull out the barbs as he would get rid of a fly, and then spurred by the fresh pain pranced around as upon his first entrance, the banderilleros in the meantime teasing him on all sides with their banners. Sometimes barbs containing fireworks were employed, and when thrust into the hide of the bull a series of explosions followed, adding to his anger, pain, and fright. None of the barbs retained their upright position beyond a few seconds, but hung down and flopped over his bloody neck with each motion of his body. A sure foot, a sturdy hand, a correct eye, and an active mind were essential for safety in the use of the barbed darts. Once a banderillero slipped and went down at the very feet of the bull, which rolled him over, or the man rolled himself over so as to leave his back up. His associates instantly drew the bull away and the banderillero retired from the ring exhibiting a white flag in the rear. Upon another occasion the banderillero failed to thrust in his darts and fell. The bull made a dash at him and rolled him over with his horns, but was at once drawn away by the others. The banderillero quickly recovered his feet, and the next minute did his work successfully, though the audience excitedly shouted "No" when he resumed his position and challenged the bull. After a bull had been worried with darts six or eight minutes the bugle again sounded and the espada advanced—he with the woman's knot of hair—bearing a scarlet cloth about four feet square and a long straight slim sword. Sometimes the bull was so discouraged that the bright cloth flirted in his face failed to stir him to another attack, but usually it appeared as a new enemy or a deeper insult that only an application of horns could avenge. So he followed it, first to one side and then the other, until perhaps he zigzagged entirely across the ring like a dancing trick horse, paying no attention to the man himself, though not more than three feet away, but keeping his wicked eye riveted upon the blood-red flag. After a great deal too much of that, the espada taking a careful aim straight to the front sheathed his sword to the hilt between the bull's shoulders just at the base of the neck. If the right spot was touched the bull immediately humped his back, the blood flowed rapidly from his nose and mouth, and in a moment or two he fell to the ground. The last actor then appeared, called the puntillero, who with a short sharp instrument stabbed the bull just back of the horns so as to touch the spinal cord and cause instant death. Then the performers all proceeded to the front of the President's box and bowed low in token of duty courageously and manfully performed; and while thus certifying to their own prowess, the gates opened for one of the mule teams gaily caparisoned and jingling numerous joyous bells. The team being attached to the horns of the dead bull, the band struck up a victorious strain, the mules were lashed to the jump, and the carcass was dragged to the slaughter yard outside for cutting up. Then another bull was promptly admitted and the entire performance repeated—the usual number of bulls for one afternoon being six.

It was not the proper thing for the espada to thrust the bull except the latter was advancing; hence it was rare to hit the right spot at the first attempt—one of them making no less than ten thrusts before downing the bull. Sometimes the sword struck a bone, and fell to the ground, as it was not part of the espada's business to remain in front of a wounded bull long enough to withdraw the blade; at other times, though well driven into the bull it was pointed wrong, so that the wound was only mortal through the slow process of bleeding to death. Then the bull would slowly walk along the side of the fence, the handle of the sword protruding from his back, exhibiting no disposition to fight and only seeking to avoid his tormentors. In such cases the sword would be recovered by two men sweeping his back with one of the long cloths, which caught the hilt in its course and dragged it upon the ground. If not killed at the first thrust there was little probability of further resistance from the bull; and as it was unpopular, even if allowed, to strike him when quiet, it became very tedious; yet frequently the only way to end the unequal conflict was to strike him when still and bleeding to death.

Generally the bull seemed anxious to escape after the first six or eight minutes of teasing. On first entering from darkness to light, with the pain of the entrance rosette fresh, he usually bounded around so as to make things very lively and everyone clear the fence but the picadores. After a few minutes fighting nothing more substantial than rage and wind, his aggressive disposition disappeared and his sallies were produced by teasing. Occasionally a bull attempted to jump the five-foot fence. One did so twice—first getting his forelegs over and then tumbling the rest of his body after them heels over head. One bull was partly over when a spectator behind the fence seized him by the horns, struck him with his straw hat, and shouted in his ear so successfully that with the assistance of others who ran up, he pushed him back into the ring. Once or twice a bull cleared the fence without losing his feet, and one did so unexpectedly, when the narrow alley was occupied by quite a number of persons who had clambered down from the seats above. The bull was amongst them before they could all leap the fence, and he assisted one who was partly over and sent him sprawling into the ring—the big audience cheering for the bull. One animal entered the ring without his rosette. He appeared to have escaped from his pen, and beholding daylight through the cracks of the door leading to the arena, dashed against it and broke off the top board. Then seeing daylight plainer he made another burst, at which his head went through by knocking off another board. The third time his forelegs mounted those still in place, and breaking them off, he entered the ring at a lope, but was very sorry for it soon afterwards, for he had not the slightest chance. He followed the rags hither and thither, first one and then another, without continuity of purpose, like some men with little tenacity, accomplishing nothing at anything, but wearing themselves out. If the bull knew enough to tackle the men instead of the rags, and would adhere to one until he had finished him, there would be a sudden cessation of bullfighting, a good many well-shaped fellows would be searching for other jobs. The audience was liberal with applause or disapproval. Once when a bull was assaulting a horse, the picador reached over and pulled from the bull the rosette that had been thrust in his back at the entrance. This being secured by a barb in his tough hide required several seconds, and the bull's horns pressing the horse all the time, the audience went wild with delight. The picador doffed his hat and rode around the ring bowing to the crowd, which flung him cigars and hats by the score. The cigars were gathered for him by the negro attendants, and the hats flung back. It appeared to be considered an honor to venture one's hat into the arena during a contest and get it safely back again. One espada did the work of the puntillero with his sword after the bull had received his death wound, but was still on his feet. The bull sprang into the air from all fours, and while up nearly turned a somersault by kicking with each leg in a different direction. At this exploit hats and cigars were showered into the ring without regard to expense. After the audience had been wearied with the delayed death of one bull, an espada dispatched the next at the first thrust; which was greeted with such cheers that the President signified that the bull should be his. Thereupon he stopped its passage to the butcher yard, severed a bloody ear, saluted the president, and then flung the ear into the midst of the audience, where doubtless it would have been scrambled for had the benches permitted. The espada also received a liberal contribution of hats and cigars. Disapproval was indicated by shouts of "no" and other words of direct significance, and once by the flinging of cushions into the ring. Some of the audience had brought small cheaply-stuffed bags to soften their seats, and on that occasion—the sport being nearly over—they dispensed with the bags to express disapproval. A bull was also the recipient of applause or disapproval as well as the men, and one, which had inherited its disposition to fight beyond a threatening shake of the head, was ordered out by the President after several minutes of shouting by the people. Then ensued more fun. The bull wanted to get away somewhere badly enough but on passing through the gate that had been opened for him to the slaughter yard, he detected an odor stronger than a hint, and hastened back before the gate could be closed. Then a darkey lassoed him and they attempted to pull him out, but he would not go. Then they lassoed him a second time, one rope being over his horns and the other over his head; and by chocking him nearly to death, and twisting his tail all out of shape, they finally succeeded in getting rid of him. All this time the audience was pelting him with pared oranges; until more than a hundred lay around, which the darkeys then picked up and threw over the fence.

The general impression left on the writer's mind, while entirely antagonistic to the sport, was moderated from former views. First, the approval of the ladies, as illustrated by their attendance, was not general, there being not to exceed fifty in an audience of 5,000, and doubtless many of them were foreigners like Judie, who by the way was the first lady present on the second Sunday the men attended. Though the audience indulged in much shouting there was no disturbance, which in a sport of such general demoralizing tendency was deemed an improvement on the probable outcome of such a gathering in the States. Third: the people looked upon the suffering of dumb brutes with indifference, but there were also fine grades or distinctions of expression which indicated a finer sensibility than was expected in such an audience and in such a sport. This was illustrated in the cheering of a gallant effort by a bull, or a hazardous one by a man. Fourth: They exhibited humanity by objecting to a second attempt of one of the banderilleros to thrust his darts into a bull after having fallen at the first effort, and when it was presumed that he might not be sufficiently collected to repeat the effort without unusual personal danger. Fifth: they exhibited a certain sense of fair play or rather disapproval of mere slaughter, by hooting a thrust by an espada when the bull was quiet. The cruelty to the horses and the torturing of the bulls themselves were the inexcusable features. Yet in the United States practices equally as demoralizing and outrageous had often been tolerated: The assaults on the Chinese in Denver and elsewhere were far more damnable; variety exhibitions had been given in Denver much more demoralizing, and farther reaching; some of the outrages tolerated at the polls in Denver had been more disastrous to the institutions which make an American look upon the Stars and Stripes in a foreign part with a thrill of pride, than bull fighting is to any Cuban or Spanish principles of government. Finally, it was said that the bull fighters were all Spaniards and the Cubans approved of none of that kind of sports except cock fighting.

The effect of the tournaments upon the Denver party was marked. The ladies took back seats when the blood began to flow, claiming that though forced to attend they could not be obliged to look; and faithfully adhered to their declaration, though occasionally standing on tiptoe to peer over the heads of the natives who had gathered between them and the box. It was also observed that a few evenings later they almost wore the gentlemen out while dickering with an Obispo street dealer for some souvenir fans representing handsome Spaniards sticking their swords into graceful Cuban bulls. Nephew Fuller was so much affected that his appetite for fresh meat was utterly destroyed, and he refused to partake of any more juicy steak while remaining with the party at the San Carlos table; but it was possible that weariness of abstinence hastened his departure to another hotel, where he could indulge in fresh meat without being subjected to inquisitive remarks.

NEIGHBORING TOWNS.

To visit one of the smaller cities in the neighborhood of Havana was to see them all in a general way. Their narrow streets were lined with the same class of houses—one story stone, chimneyless, dirty, variegated, stucco-cracked, the streets were rocky, gullied and narrow-sidewalked; the children dirty, naked, or half clad; the women running to the window bars to stare at the stranger as if he was the prisoner and they the spectators; free odors at every waft of air irrespective of taste, goats and kids browsing on bones and cactus; and old negro women, sometimes with tattooed faces, the apparent age of centuries bending their backs, plodding through the streets leaning on stout cudgels, big bundles on their heads, and the short stumps of black cigars between their enormous flabby lips.

Guanabacoa was reached by crossing the ferry to Regla and thence fifteen minutes by rail. At the Havana end of the ferry little brass medals or checks were purchased for twenty cents the round trip, and which were deposited upon entering the ship at a self-registering gate. Upon reaching Regla cars were taken, but no tickets required, the medals having paid for the through trip. The country was rather pretty and fairly cultivated, a pair of oxen and an iron-pointed crooked stick doing the ploughing. Fields were separated by low hedges of wild pineapple, with occasionally a stone wall. The principal tree was the royal palm, but there were no forests. At Guanabacoa depot sufficient Spanish was resurrected to engage a victoria for an hour, for three dollars, and with the ladies on the back seat, Mike and Roger opposite, and Cook perched beside the driver, they got their money's worth and were glad when they returned. How the women and children and negroes hastened to the doors and iron bars to look! Those who arrived first beckoned those behind to hurry up, and they all laughed in great glee at the sight. Their mirth was apparently in derision, which was concluded to have been at the simplicity of the Americans in hiring a carriage to see such a place as Guanabacoa. The city was said to contain 10,000 people, and the visitors wondered what it was built for.

There were said to have been some springs and baths there, but the people evidently had no use for them and had forgotten their existence.

Regla also received a courteous call from the two couples, which fact became a standing joke thereafter whenever a member of the party became so reckless as to express a wish to go somewhere. They wandered in a lost kind of way through its narrow streets, and were again made to feel that American ladies and gentlemen had never before been beheld in Regla, for the one-story dwellings had their windows crowded with staring women and children, white, black, and yellow, as if the great giascutis had just arrived. An old negro woman picking up banana peel and cigar stubs from the street was the most hideous looking creature they ever beheld—a hag from the crown of her head to the sole of her foot—a veritable ogress of the Arabian Nights—whose countenance was more ugly than was ever invented for carnival monstrosities. She had only one eye, but that was as large as two and as wicked as ten. She had an immense bloated face, and sucking the stub of a cigar in her hideous lips, formed a horrible-looking object that was supposed to have been originally fashioned after the Great Creator himself! Ye Gods! What evolution! After studying human nature unadorned in Regla's byways they wandered into the sugar "almacen de Catalina," an immense room with iron roof and pillars, capable of containing many thousands—aye, hundreds of thousands of barrels. It was nearly empty, but in one part were a half dozen Chinamen, naked to the waist, hauling bags of sugar to the top of a large pile, and whose expressionless faces and perspiration-begrimed bodies were slavelike in the extreme. The Cubans superintending the work politely uncovered as the party passed. Near the ferry were a number of men engaged in a ropewalk, and close by, on the very brink of the waves, by a blacksmith shop, was a little garden from which a man picked them some fruit and flowers, and a leaf from a shrub that from its odor appeared to be allspice.

Marianao, another little town, with some alleged springs and a stone bridge, was reached by rail after taking carriage to the depot by way of the calzada Reina and paseo de Tacon, not far from the Plaza de Toros—the round trip fare by rail being ninety cents. The signal for the starting of the train was the ringing of the dinner bell by a negro trainman in lieu of the American "All Aboard," by the conductor. They passed through a number of small towns on the way, the principal being Fuentes Grande. Marianao possessed one street and a half, through which they rode to "La Lisa" hotel, kept by a brother of their St. Charles landlord Rebozo, who could talk no English, but tried very hard to understand their Spanish. He protected them from the rapacity of the driver of their carriage who insisted on three dollars for an hour's drive, and sent for another which cost two. In it they rode a mile beyond and saw a sugar plantation and a pineapple field. The pines were quite thickly planted, and their appearance much like the spreading end of the apple itself, but from two to four feet long. Some were green and others of a pinkish hue. The plants bore their fruit on stems or spines shooting up from the center, and which was in every stage from infancy the size of a walnut, to maturity. At the old house at the end of Pineapple Avenue, where an aged negro couple were found, Mike purchased a large dark green pineapple, which they assured him was ready for eating notwithstanding its color. Near the very attractive road over which they drove was a beautiful grove of mango trees, resembling, except in the color of their reddish blossoms, the American chestnuts. Many handsome royal palms also abounded—one a novel thing—six inches in diameter a few feet from the ground, and at least fifteen inches thirty feet higher.

Vedada and Chorrera were neat, quiet, and attractive in appearance. They consisted of a single long street by the sea shore, and a few short streets attached, and were reached in twenty minutes by dummy cars from La Punta. The neat one-story houses were surrounded with attractive gardens, and comprised the summer residences of the wealthier Havanese. The gulf shore was low and formed of the usual honeycombed limestone of Cuba, and along which they wandered for an hour gathering shells and sponge. On their return Mike deserted at La Punta on an alleged search after Mrs. Warner's baby.

Anna and Roger one hot morning took street cars to a suburban part of the city called "Cerro," but saw nothing to justify a repetition of the visit.

February fourteenth, after digesting valentines and cucumbers, a second visit was made to Chorrera, the first site of Havana. The dummy train was long and every available foot of space occupied, many going to the cemetery, and others to the Vedada baseball grounds, which by the way, were excellent. On arriving at Chorrera a boatman accosted them, and while slowly arriving at an understanding in Spanish relative to the ride they proposed to take up the river, he hailed a passing young fellow who knew English, to interpret; and through whose assistance a bargain was soon made for four dollars paper. On thanking the interpreter he politely informed the party that they were "very excusable," which well illustrated the size of his English. The boatman earned his money by rowing them two or three miles up the Aladama river to an attractive cascade, where they landed on a little island, cut canes, and cracked inferior nuts beneath a large almond tree. The river was fifty to a hundred feet wide, deep in places, shallow in others, and with many large rocks reaching to the surface, though generally reedy at bottom. The water, however, was clear, and from a bridge beneath which they passed were men spearing large fish, while others were hooking from the shore. The event of the day was the cutting of jointed canes, and only after some time was it discovered that one with a handle was to be obtained from a limb instead of a root. Returning down the river they arrived at an old wall eight feet high, by the side of which grew a cane tree, and into the tree Mike successfully climbed, but at great expense of muscle and cuticle. Returning to Chorrera they camped on the veranda of a public house to trim their canes and destroy a quart of limonada apiece.

Two or three miles west of the city was the principal burial place called the "Cementario de Colon." Taking the Principe street car and alighting at the terminus on paseo Tacon, they walked to a small posada at the foot of Principe to await the arrival of the "bus." After disposing of the usual quantity of poor lemonade without ice, the gentlemen played a game of billiards while the ladies studied the poetry of nature as illustrated in an unclad baby. The Cuban billiard table was about twice the area of the American, while the balls were four inches in diameter, and the cues weighed two pounds. The game was pool, and the marker raked the fallen pins within reach with the bridge, and chalked the game on the cushion. The "bus" was a square box on wheels, with scant room for six, and drawn by a pair of horses just ready to graduate into the bull ring. The cemetery was surrounded by a high wall and iron fence in alternate sections, and had a massive arched stone entrance. A building on the left inside contained a priest or two ready for work. There were many beautiful and elaborate marble monuments, and others of stucco that looked equally as well at a short distance. The private tombs, mostly of stucco, were of graceful designs. The graves were usually cement vaults, covered with marble slabs in various forms, the cross predominating. Very elegant designs of beadwork were common, while other lots contained vases of flowers of considerable value. The main vault was 200 feet long, with three tiers of receptacles on each side, and numbering about 600 in all. After descending into this underground city of the dead, and treading its gloomy avenue, they returned to the city with feelings of relief.

MISCELLANEOUS HAVANA INCIDENTS.

One morning the party took carriages to La Punta and then walked to the baths known as Camp Elysees. These were excavations of different sizes in the solid rock on the shore of the Gulf, with a wall left at the sea front, but containing holes or gaps to admit the fresh water by every wave. Over the excavations was a roof but the sides were uncovered. The sea broke into the baths with a rush and surge that presented a spirited scene, and at times caused the visitors to draw back more rapidly than the great crabs that clung to the sides of the excavations. While there, a New York steamer entering port near by made a beautiful addition to the scene.

Passing the Captain General's palace at the Plaza de Armas one day, the gentlemen pointed to themselves and then inside, and the guard nodding an affirmative; they entered the court to examine a statue of Columbus, but made no further investigation.

One evening they strolled out to capture some brilliant-hued flowers from the plaza in front of the palace, for the pleasure of the ladies, and while awaiting increased darkness they went onto the Cathedral to ascertain if its towers were in danger of falling down; and then before sufficient darkness to justify an attempt upon the main object of the raid a heavy rain began to fall, which obliged them to take refuge beneath the overhanging top and capacious boot of a carriage and return to the hotel.

A sign that English was spoken at a nursery near the Marianao depot induced Anna and Roger to call. The latter accosted a pleasant-faced woman at the door with "Habla V. Ingles?" to which she laughed and said, "No, Señor," and retired to call the man who did. While he was gathering roses Roger and the lady made a little headway in Spanish, and she exhibited a midget of a humming bird not over an inch in length. The bird and a bashful naked jet black boy of five or six, who stood in an inner doorway sucking his thumb, were the principal objects of interest observed.

Roger telegraphed home one day for news, and learned in reply the next day that Alice was down with inflammatory rheumatism, which called for more telegrams and an order for nurses. Telegraph rates to Denver were sixty cents a word, gold, and dates, initials, address, and everything but punctuation marks was charged for at the same rate.

Near the close of their visit they met interpreter Smyrk of the Telegrafo, who appeared actually thunderstruck to learn that they had remained all that time at the San Carlos. He felt more incensed than ever that Rendon had "gotten away" with them, and declared him the worst runner he had to compete with.

With Rendon they visited the grounds of the Captain General's summer residence near Principe, and just outside the city limits. Carriage drivers could therefore fix their own rates, and as they proposed to charge two dollars each, Rendon punished them by alighting the party at the Marianao depot at fifty cents as fixed by law, and walking the short distance remaining. The grounds were approached by a handsome avenue from the

Paseo Tacon, and contained several others that were very attractive, such as royal palms, bananas, almonds, etc. The royal palms were especially choice, their trunks being smooth and regular for fifty or sixty feet, and surmounted with the usual gracefully waving palm branches. A novel production, commonly known as the "monkey tree," was four or five feet in diameter at the ground, and only a foot ten or twelve feet higher. None regretted that the Captain General's house was closed, as like the grounds it was not so well kept as might have been—too many muskets, and too few brooms and spades.

The afternoon before leaving Cuba they took the two o'clock train for Marianao with C.A. Raymond and his party, in company. At Marianao they engaged carriages for the Toledo sugar factory two miles distant, and the road to which passed through the canefields, which resembled a sea of growing corn fodder. A gate at the outskirts was kept by an attendant who admitted no visitors without a pass.

The machinery of the mill was extensive and expensive. Many ox-carts were employed in hauling cane from the fields to a long tramway, upon which the cane was thrown from the carts to a depth of about fifteen inches. At least a hundred feet of tramway was thus kept constantly loaded and slowly passing forward to the crusher, beneath which a great quantity of juice was steadily flowing, and where a perspiring negro stood skimming off the scum. The cane was then elevated and passed through a second crusher, after which it was spread over the fields to dry for fuel, a good sized farm for a Yankee was thus covered with the chewed cane. The elaborate process of boiling the juice was examined through to tasting the syrup and sugars, which was accompanied with polite comments in English on the big bare feet of the Negroes who stood in the sugar while shoveling it up. The odor of the hot syrup was akin to sickening, and they were glad to wander over to the locked gates of the negro quarters, and from thence to the cool aguadiente stills, to remove the taste by a sip of the crystal rum. On their return a balky horse in the narrow road delayed them just long enough to miss the train, which hurt their feelings and soured them against other travelers not attached to their own party.

Matanzas.

Monday the eighth of February was fixed for visiting Matanzas sixty miles eastward on the Gulf coast. Promptly at two o'clock Mike carved his big green pineapple, and declared that it was the best he had tasted since he was a boy. Anna devoured her portion with appetite equal to the others, and after the last morsel had been picked up, innocently remarked that she wished it had been a water-melon!

They took the ferry at 3:30, and enjoyed a few minutes on the Regla side noting the motley passengers just alighting from the inbound train, with sacks of fighting cocks and other poultry, and all sorts of contrivances for the transportation of baggage, bags predominating. The ride through the country was quite attractive, the noble avenue of royal palms being especially fixed in the memory. Some of these were a half mile in length without a tree being out of line. The palms also grew wild in a scattered way, but never appeared as forests. A very pretty scene was a village below the road in a little valley, the thatched huts of palm peeping out from groves of bananas as in pictures of interior Africa. It was nearly dusk when the abrupt Pan mountains of Matanzas were skirted, and half-past six on arriving at the San Carlos hotel near the San Juan river, and in driving to which they were unmercifully bumped over the rough pavement. The San Carlos of Matanzas was years before owned by a dealer in African slaves, who had a passage from near the river to an underground depot, where he secreted them until a favorable opportunity to run them into the interior. The hotel dining room was upon the ground floor next the street, and light and air were admitted through customary gratings. The second story was floored with red tile, including the sleeping rooms, which were furnished with the usual canvas beds, except that Mike was a little set up over the possession of springs; but as the regulation allowance of blankets was adhered to, Mike wanted to exchange with someone the next night. After supper on the evening of arrival the gentlemen patronized some little half-clad negro bootblacks, who then adjourned to the sidewalk across the narrow street, to gamble for the money. During the operation an annoyed attendant from a drug store appeared with a two-horse syringe and showered them with a bath, whereupon the most enterprising of the boys seized the funds and started to Canada with all the others in pursuit. Before supper, feeling fatigued with the hot afternoon ride, and Mike expressing a desire to close out his small stock of Denver whisky, the gentlemen worried down a small swallow each and said nothing about it to the ladies. After supper Jane declared that someone had been at the whisky flask, but the men, while agreeing to the fact, professed entire ignorance. The ladies therefore, in order to protect the chambermaid from suspicion thus aroused by attention having been directed to the matter, were finally obliged to confess that they were the guilty parties themselves, and had both taken a little for Anna's ear-ache; whereupon the men toed the mark and acknowledged having taken a trifle on the same account. They were unable to determine, however, which couple got at it first.

Tuesday morning at nine o'clock the two best volantes in Matanzas pulled up at the door just as they sat down to breakfast. The vehicles were bright, the manes and tails of the horses neatly braided, the silver-buckled harness clean and new, the caleseros clad in white pants and jackets, and all making very nobby turnouts. Mike and Jane led off with a pair of mustangs, and Roger, Anna and Rendon with some whites. The ride for a mile was along the shell-strewn beach, made additionally agreeable by a refreshing breeze wafted across the bay. They then turned into a guava country by a hilly road paved by Nature with great boulders, and where they realized the adaptability of a volante, back against the seat of which they could repose with entire freedom from disagreeable jolting. The caves of Bellamar were about two and a half miles from the city, the entrance being by a pair of steep narrow stairs in the middle of a low building erected over the spot. After the men had divested themselves of coats, vests, collars and cuffs, and the ladies had shed all that propriety allowed, an attendant with an immense torch or candle of yellow wax, led in the descent. The atmosphere at once became hot and stifled and the perspiration commenced to roll. After descending some fifty feet by two or three flights of stairs, they proceeded along an irregular passage that had once been the course of a subterranean stream. It averaged twenty-five feet in width and fifteen high, but occasionally was so low as to make stopping requisite. The route gradually descended as they slowly proceeded, examining the stalactites and stalagmites that abounded on every hand, and all of which were somewhat blackened by smoke. At one or two places the torches being held behind some large stalactites exhibited their transparency; and at another, a half mile from the surface, they quaffed to the health of those they left behind them from a sweet though warmish spring that flowed from beneath a cluster of overhanging columns. As there was a stall in one corner of the building above the cave for the sale of specimens at fancy prices, visitors were strictly forbidden to help themselves to any of the thousands of glittering crystals that sparkled from the roof; but on returning to the hotel it was discovered that each member of the party had several very fair specimens. Upon explanation it appeared that they were examining them at different parts of the low roof, when the guide was well in advance, and accidentally the specimens broke off in their hands. The coincidence struck them as being quite remarkable, to say the least. The largest chamber in the cave was near the entrance, and while the balance was not grand, it was decidedly elegant. They reached the end, a mile distant, in three quarters of an hour, and returned in half the time partly by another route. The ladies stood the severe trip and hot air admirably, as in every other case where their mettle was tested; and on returning to the surface all promptly resumed their outer clothing, paid nine dollars paper for their entertainment, spent a half hour for cooling, cut some guava canes in the shrubbery, and returned to the hotel for a nap.

At 3:15 they resumed their volantes and proceeded to a high promontory of land overlooking the city and harbor on one hand and the Yumuri valley on the other. The valley or basin was about five by ten miles, everywhere divided into farms and dotted with waving palms. Upon the summit of the promontory was a chapel erected by citizens of Montserrat in Catalonia, Spain; and within which was a model in cork of the home mountain and home church. The gray color and shape of the cork were almost identical with the rocky cliffs, a piece of which was exhibited for comparison. In the chapel also attention was directed to a cabinet of offerings to "Nuestra Señora de Montserrat," consisting of silver representations of human arms, legs, heads, hands and other parts of the body. These offerings were to secure for afflicted friends the gracious intercession of "our lady," and they indicated the particular part of the human anatomy which needed her special attention. A variety of interesting church trinkets manufactured in Barcelona was also exhibited and samples sold to the members of the party. The man in

charge also insisted on showing them all the church robes; and a life-size figure of the Madonna that adorned a niche above the altar; and as there was nothing more, leading them to his wife and children in a little house adjoining. There he produced a registry book containing an invitation in Spanish and English for all visitors to Montserrat to inscribe therein their names and what they thought of the charming spot. Many pages were thus filled—many with addresses alone, and others conveying their sentiments at length, both in prose and poetry, in Spanish and English. The expressions of thought were mostly fanciful as though carried away by the beauty of the scene; others were merely statements that the writers considered themselves well repaid for the visit; while others yet were indecent and profane as shown by the following two samples:

"This is a damn beautiful hill and a damn fine valley. I recommend the virgin for her miraculous virtue. Drunk as hell and glad of it. <u>Kentucky</u>."

—"Being in company with the above named gentleman I am of the same opinion, only adding thereto, that being a Southern man from the word 'go,' I here on the beautiful hill give three cheers for the bonnie blue flag, and may all Yankees go to the Devil—Boston and down-eastern fellows especially."

It was remarkable that they had sufficient sense to omit their names. After registration, giving the man a paper dollar and his children some punched silver, and then going out to see his goats and lean over the wall surrounding the small summit, they drove across the asphaltum pavement on their descent to the city. On the outskirts they stopped at a beautiful dwelling with charming grounds surrounding, comprising the summer residence of a wealthy sugar planter then living in the city, and were accorded the privilege of being escorted through the place. The family living rooms were all on the first floor, and were simplicity and elegance combined. Two of them were floored with several varieties of native woods, such as mahogany, tamarind, etc., combined in mosaic designs; and one of the back rooms opening from a bedroom and dining porch, was fitted as a chapel, with a costly altar and figures of the holy personages. The beds were such as the party had already become familiar with. Driving through the streets they were again the objects of great curiosity on the part of women and girls—the whole population seeming to have thronged the barred windows to obtain a sight, and at one of which no less than seven heads were counted. The negro boys in the streets satisfied their juvenile curiosity with running two blocks to ride one by clinging to the rear of the volantes. Before reaching the hotel they halted at a photographer's to negotiate for their pictures in the volantes, but as he demanded twenty-five dollars for each, and he objected to paying him for his entire establishment, they bade him buenos dias.

The next morning they entered the volantes for the third time and went into the country about five miles to a coffee plantation. On the way through the suburbs of the city they noted as on previous occasions a number of fences built with railroad rails imbedded in the tops of concrete posts. The ride to

the plantation in the cool of the morning was delightful, the country road being walled, and lined in many places with noble rows of royal palms, whilst among the trees and shrubbery was more music of birds than they had before listened to. The road was in one place very rocky and steep so that Roger and Rendon alighted to lessen the load. A few moments later the shaft horse stumbled and the volante commenced a retrograde movement which was continued until the horse was pulled completely down and the wheels run against the bank. Anna in the meantime went out like a deer fleeing for liberty, and the trio walked to the summit of the hill while the fallen horse was unharnessed and put upon his feet again by the two caleseros. The coffee trees or shrubs were five or six feet high with long branches, and bore round berries in hulls containing two kernels each. While some strong coffee was being made for them at the dwelling they speculated on the naked girl baby, a number of lean flea-bitten dogs, cats, and kittens, and other "cosas de Cuba" that abounded in the neighborhood. The old native in charge accompanied them to the orange trees, from which he furnished a generous supply, and Rendon imposed upon the ladies a beautiful sour one the character of which was not exposed by its appearance. Near the house was a larger tree like the apple in shape, from which they gathered a handful of green tamarinds. On the other side was a large area devoted to the banana, and just beyond a field of cane, but the latter was too sickish sweet to be palatable to stomachs in daily contact with oil and garlic. On their return to Matanzas they cut a supply of canes from the cane trees along the road, and having partaken of dinner, they settled their bill and departed, Mike and Roger an hour in advance for a stretch along the seashore for shells, and the ladies with Rendon and the baggage. Matanzas was agreed to be a pretty city, and many Americans visited it, amongst them at the time of this story being a party of the name of "Fuller," and wife, of Denver, but not at the San Carlos. At the depot Mike and Roger spent an hour in watching the lottery dealers and beggars, and especially the rivalry between two of the latter—a man and a woman—as to which should first reach the side of each newly-arriving carriage. Whenever the woman seemed to have a change of securing a trifle, the man invariably shoved his hand in ahead, and seemed to be the most persistent beggar that ever was. He might have been dumb for all the talking he did, but during the intervals between the arrival of carriages he would stand at a barred window of the reception room, thrust his long hand through, fix his eyes on someone inside, and thus stand and stare without a wink or a waver beyond a demanding motion of the appealing digits, for five minutes or more. The return to Havana in a full coach was so hot and tiresome that they began to seriously hunger for the United States.

Preparing for Departure.

The party having been in Cuba four weeks had peeped at the elephant wherever he was found on exhibition; so that his colossal proportions had gradually diminished to those of an ordinary mouse; while their dissatisfaction with the San Carlos hotel had developed from the size of a mouse to that of an elephant. These changes, coupled with an increasing dislike for anything possessing a flavor of Havana, brought them all down simultaneously with a raging fever to get away. Therefore visiting Lawton Brothers on the 11th of February and learning that the Mascotte staterooms were all engaged until the 17th, they at once engaged two of the four remaining; and a day or two later, deeming it fair to notify Rendon of their intended departure, he promptly met them half way by soliciting their consent to a change of their rooms for the few remaining days to the next story above, so that he could accommodate other parties about to arrive for a stay of some months. But as they were inwardly growling at the charge at full rates while visiting Matanzas, in opposition to agreement, they declined the invitation with thanks. Inquiring then about the regulation of passports, Rendon informed them that the expense would be three dollars each, which he offered to have attended to with his usual courtesy, but having obtained a grain of information on the same subject at the steamship office, Mike acted as agent and saved $2.75 each. The morning of the last day but one was employed in calling upon those whose acquaintance they had made, like Kicherer and Wilson, and bidding them goodbye; and upon the last evening the gentlemen made a final call upon Mrs. Warner's baby and took the mother's remembrances to friends in Denver. At the depot of Señor Alvarez they laid in such stock of cigars as they thought might pass the customs blockade at Tampa. The last evening they occupied in disposing of their Spanish money, stocking up with guava jelly and alleged tamarinds, and settling their bills, which included three dollars a couple for getting on board. This all arranged, the men retired into a corner to consider the advisability of chartering a sailing vessel the ensuing Winter, and with their entire families spending three or four months amongst the many small islands off the southeastern coast of the United States. The suggestions were received with favor, and Mike arranged to take a camera along so as to be independent of the natives who might want to charge twenty-five dollars for each picture. They packed their trunks and attempted to retire early, but a delay in the return of Roger's washing gave an extra hour to bestow upon Isabel and the mulatto bootblack such rare curiosities as they could not transport, including a leaky cocoanut that had been originally destined for one end of the parlor mantel at home.

HAVANA TO TAMPA.

At seven o'clock on the 17th of February they partook of "café con leche y bizcochos" at the hotel for the last time, and after bidding a hasty farewell all around, set out on their homeward journey with satisfaction at least equal to that with which they had arrived. The clouds had borne evidence of tears from the earliest streak of light, and after they had spent a half hour on the wharf awaiting the loading of trunks, and finally crowded into the boat themselves so that there could no longer be a doubt of their intention to depart, the indications of grief commenced to fall in a decisive manner. There was no wind for the sail, the boat was low in the water, the space between the awning was crowded with passengers, and the baggage was piled so high in front as to prevent much use of the oars. The rain continued to fall, so that Roger was obliged to unfurl his umbrella at the end of the awning, and from which the water streamed into Mike's coat pocket. After an hour's race with a deceased snail on shore and in which the latter was victor, they were taken in tow by a passing boat and in due time reached the Mascotte, where was much confusion incident upon a crowded boat and the approach of the departing hour. Rendon accompanied them on board, and after waiting a reasonable length of time for the bestowal of any parting gifts, took his departure in the "Dos Amigos" with mutual expressions of obligation. Upon interviewing the young old Purser he relinquished their passports that he had deposited at the city office for examination and delivered their stateroom tickets entitling each couple to two "births," which was a trifle alarming until they discovered that he was deficient in orthography. Their rooms were on deck in near proximity to those of ex-governor English of Connecticut, H.B. Plant, the owner of the boat, and Mrs. Frank Leslie, who had been bumming around Havana for two weeks. Plant was a sensible-looking man; English was a vain-glorious old turkey-cock; and Mrs. Leslie was seeking to keep up an impression that she was young and attractive. A little after ten the Mascotte started slowly out and the passengers waved their handkerchiefs in response to numerous salutes from the San Carlos balconies and other buildings along the shore. Morro was passed at ten-twenty, and then the whole force of the Mascotte engines was applied, and she tore through the water like mad. The dark blue surface of the Gulf Stream, though seeming fair from shore, was found to be quite rough, but all partook of dinner except Roger, who decided to let well enough alone and nibble a San Carlos biscuit. Rain fell at intervals through the day, and they were rejoiced to sight United States possessions at half past four, even such a semi-Cuban port as Key West. Apparently the same crowd of persons lined the dock as before, and a half hour was enjoyed in watching three amphibious fellows swimming around in the water and diving for nickels and dimes flung them by the passengers. Roger went ashore and wired home for a message to meet him at Tampa; and again met Judge Locke, who spent a half hour with them on the boat. Departing for Tampa the 6:10 and all retiring early, they slept well through the night. At breakfast the next morning they had turned toward the shore, and at ten-thirty had sighted the transfer steamer Margaret steaming down Tampa bay. Then ensued various scientific methods of disposing of cigars—each passenger having had to certify to the Purser what dutiable goods he possessed, which list was turned over to the collector of the port, and the baggage searched in the order in which the names were enrolled. Mike covered his box of gold leaf cigars with various duds, after first rubbing the cover with dirt to give it an aged appearance; and Roger stowed his away in his hip pockets, which as he was rather thin, gave him a fairly plump appearance, and was therefore rather an improvement than otherwise. The satchels and trunks were all put on board the Margaret before passengers were permitted to transfer, and then everything being badly mixed, much grumbling ensued during the inspection, which took place while steaming up the bay, so that passengers might be ready on arrival to take the noon train for Jacksonville if they desired. Mike struck an inspector who was easily imposed upon by his venerable appearance and permitted him to slip by untaxed; while Roger fell to the lot of one who believed in making a semblance of performing duty, and therefore taxed him two dollars and thirty-five cents on what he admitted to be in his possession, but made no examination beyond barely opening the trunk and satchels. Roger was of the opinion that he might have smuggled a trunk full of dutiable goods undetected, unless the knowledge of guilt should have so stamped itself on his phiz as to have given the whole thing away. Or he might have chalked his baggage himself and hustled it ashore with that which bore the inspectors' marks.

TAMPA AGAIN.

The Denver baggage was passed just as they reached the wharf, and just as landlord Franz of the Palmetto arrived with a telegram for Roger that all were well at home and nurses discharged. They proceeded at once to the hotel, where the old guests received them cordially and kept them busy the remainder of the day replying to questions relating to Havana. Dinner was ready shortly after arrival, at which they were as elated as newly naturalized Irishmen voting the first time for Aldermen. Everything tasted good, particularly the pie, which was an unknown luxury in Cuba. Mike and Roger made a dash at the pickle bottle between courses, and impartially divided its contents. They were brimful of satisfaction and the Palmetto appeared for the time being as the most desirable hotel within their knowledge. Tampa was noted to have improved considerably during their absence. The cold weather having passed, the orange trees had shed their leaves and were budding anew, but the lemon trees were killed to the ground. The ladies having expressed a desire to remain a few days, and Anna having a fat poultice on each ear with a red handkerchief around her head, being unable to travel, the men decided upon some bangup Florida sport all by themselves. So in the intervals between interviews with strangers seeking information of Havana, and practicing billiards at a saloon down town, they gathered instruction on the science of hunting 'gators. Down at the dock on Sunday afternoon, while interviewing the captain of an excursion smack as to the cost of a cruise among the Bermudas and Bahamas, a native regaled them with his personal experiences with an alligator twenty-eight feet long, the head of which was severed from its body, and the next day winked and bit off a man's fingers. They politely listened with only a remark to each other that the hour was about "ten," while the native winked to the bysitters to observe how nicely he had taken them in. Relative to the proposed Atlantic voyage the ensuing Winter, the captain of the smack estimated that a vessel of sixty tons would cost, including crew, $700.00 a month—the captain $60, the mate $30, and two men $70 each; while fare for the four would aggregate $40 a month. He said a new vessel could be built in Florida for $40 a ton. Two or three times a boating a fishing excursion was taken up the Hillsborough river, which proved Jane to be the most successful fisher, she catching three cats; Mike, several crabs; and Roger nothing. Mike's "crabs" were caught with the oars while rowing down the river. The hotel gradually began to present less attractions as the dishes became more familiar and the manager's quarrels with his waiters more numerous. The darkeys no doubt gave him much annoyance, for their feet and hands were very slow, their heads very thick, their drunks very independent, and their orders never correctly delivered. For instance, when Mike first requested "fried eggs turned over," James Madison rolled his eyes in ignorant intelligence and brought eggs that had been fried on one side, then turned over and the raw side laid gently upon the slice of ham. When the proprietor's complaints admitted of a breathing spell, the men found trifles of their own to dispute upon, such as the name of the revenue collector on the transfer Margaret. Neither remembered the name, but each insisted that it was a word of a certain number of syllables, and bet their hats on the number— Mike's wager being the twenty-five dollar Panama purchased in Havana. Roger won the bet, but never secured the hat; yet he insisted that the historian should record the fact of his mortgage and announce to the people of Denver that the handsome broad-brimmed Panama sported around the streets so magnificently by Mike, really belonged to him. The party avoided political disputes with native Southerners as being useless, but one day old Doctor Crichton of Atlanta was declaiming of ante-bellum days; in which he asserted that the North was wont to insist that "a nigger was a good as a white man" and appealed to Roger in corroboration. The latter replied that he had never heard such a claim put forth, but only that a negro was entitled to the same rights and justice as a white man, whereupon the Doctor retired on the verge of disgust. Mike discovered the earliest strawberries of Spring upon the 27th of February, and promptly purchased all there were in market, namely, one pint, for fifty cents. They proved to be very palatable in connection with baked wild turkey. The Secretary of the Board of Trade called with the compliments of the President and tendered the courtesies of the organization to the gentlemen, who in due time returned the call. Mr. Raymond and his party arrived from Havana after a stormy passage of two days, about the time the gentlemen had secured rifles, after a long search, for a grand alligator jamboree at Manatee; and after the abandonment of a plan to charter the "Ada M.D.," for a party of eight, at $12.50 a day because her bottom was stove in. The day before leaving for St. Augustine they met Judge Locke on the street, who had arrived to open court, and who called in the evening for an hour's review with Roger on boyhood days. Between them they called up the old "Excelsior" boys of Manchester, noting how some had exceeded the promise of youth, and others of brighter parts had dwindled into insignificance. They referred to the physical changes also, as illustrated in a certain young man and woman, both knowing themselves and the other to possess beauty and grace, and whose determination to unite for life was successfully carried out; but now, alas! she weighing 220, and he bald headed and squatty, unrecognizable as having once been fleet and graceful, and the possessor of wavy hair that hung down to his shoulders. Young men and women rarely see those with whom they would mate as twenty-five years will leave them; and everything considered, it is fortunate they don't.

Manatee and Gators.

Having secured rifles and ammunition and left Anna and Jane to the tender mercies of each other, the gentlemen boarded the Margaret on the 22^d of February at two o'clock, in association with about fifty personages, for Havana by way of the Mascotte lying down the bay. With first officer Baury of the Mascotte, who was returning to his vessel, they conversed on the subject of an Atlantic sailing voyage, who commended it highly and expressed a desire to go in command. Upon reaching the Mascotte, the gentlemen speculated on the changes that would in a few hours cloud the spirits of the joyous throng, when they would have partaken of the delicacies of the Mascotte's tables and the briny deep began to toss its crested mane. The day being far spent, and the transfer of freight and baggage incomplete, the vessels were lashed together and steamed outward during the continuance of the transfer. Just before dusk the lashings were cast off and the steamers separated with parting whistles, and that was their last sight of the trim Mascotte. It had been declared that the Margaret would arrive at Manatee at 7 o'clock that evening, and therefore the passengers spent the time pleasantly enough watching the use of the electric light and revolving reflector from the bow in locating the buoys and fixed objects along the shore. They reached the station on the Manatee river about two miles from their destination at eight o'clock; and shortly afterwards pulled up at a wharf of familiar aspect, which upon closer inspection provide to be Palma Sola that they had passed an hour before; and it was reported that the return had been made to take the little steamer Erie in tow, which lay at Palma Sola, and belonged to Capt. Warner of the Margaret. After an hour's tedious delay, the men sat down for a game of cribbage, when it occurred to one to inquire if the boat was to lay there all night. The inquiry was made in a sportive way with no conception of its probability, so that the prompt reply in the affirmative was appalling. The Purser explained, to his own satisfaction, at least, that the lowness of the tide prevented the Margaret from reaching Manatee, but the little

Erie alongside was about to leave with the Margaret's freight and passengers. So he assisted them on board apparently rejoiced that they had kicked no more vigorously. The Erie had no cabin, and what space it had was filled with boxes of goods transferred from the Margaret. They clambered over the boxes of freight and with a disposition to make the best of a bad arrangement, resumed their game of crib on the top of a big box of codfish or dry goods by the light of a smoky kerosene lamp. The two men who constituted the crew seeming to have nothing to do but watch the game, inquiry was made as to how soon the boat was to depart. They said the fires had first to be built, and the captain being uptown to a ball they didn't think he would be back before twelve o'clock. Aha! So the feline animal had escaped? The captain up town at a ball, and his brother, the Captain of the Margaret, ditto? No wonder the tide was too low to reach Manatee! Then they sent one of the crew to the captain with their compliments and information that they were passengers who had paid for their transportation to Manatee, and they were awaiting his return from the ball to proceed on their journey. He responded that he would be back in a few minutes, but evidently some pair of lovely Florida eyes held him fast; for a little later the Purser of the Margaret appeared with information that the Erie would leave at three o'clock in the morning, and until which time they could occupy a stateroom and berths on the Margaret. Being powerless to oppose Fate they accepted the offer at eleven, slept three hours, then boarded the Erie and reached Manatee at half past four. Disembarking upon a wharf five feet in width they traversed it into the darkness until weary, when they met a man, and after squeezing without falling into the water, inquired the distance to shore, and the location of Mrs. Griffin's hotel. They were glad to learn that they had less than a quarter of a mile of wharf yet to traverse, and that the lady's front gate was at the back side of the house on the further side of the street to the left of the landing. Finding the gate without difficulty, and twisting around beneath the limbs of a groves of orange trees, the house loomed up in the darkness. With an inward prayer that the dog was tied, they mounted the porch and knocked at the door. A feminine voice responded from

within, and after a statement of their forlorn condition, directed them to open the door and enter the parlor, and their beds should soon be made ready. Then they retired once more and slept until eight o'clock, after which they searched the woods for a negro named Charles Harrison, and hired him at a dollar and a half a day to manage the boat, and take them where alligators were cheap. The owner of the long dock first sought to rent them a boat which would have capsized at the cock of a gun, and they obtained one of a much soiled doctor nearby. Then they sailed up the river, Mike fishing and shooting at intervals. He hit several 'gators that were sunning themselves on the banks, but as they quickly humped into the river, none were secured. They sailed from 11 to 2, and were then several miles from town with no return wind, so they poled down until 5, and then leaving their boat fastened to a tree, footed it. About dusk they reached the elegant plantation of Mr. Foster, whom they had met in January on the way to Jacksonville, and whose acquaintance they renewed for a minute in his fields. At Foster's they were joined by another negro with a thoughtless dog that ran hither and thither in the bushes as they proceeded toward town. It was then quite dark and Mike was absentmindedly thinking of how he had rather Charlie should pole the boat until midnight than take such a walk again, when the pup suddenly darted from the bushes directly in front of him. Mike being suddenly aroused, thought only of alligators traveling from lake to lake and up went his rifle to his shoulder with his finger on the trigger. The negro caught the click of the lock and yelled just in time to save the dog's life, or at least a cartridge. Reaching the hotel at 6:40, and partaking of a dish of fat oysters, they felt sufficiently refreshed to pursue their customary recreation with the cribbage board. The next day they hired a team to take them to Foster's, and then walked to the boat, in which they sailed three miles up the river with the same luck as before—Mike making three or four 'gators sick but getting no meat, while Roger only fired once at a bird singing on a tree as they passed. The return was without wind, so Charlie poled down to the "Castle," two miles from home, from which point they walked to the hotel at 6:35. The third day they took a wagon for some lakes a dozen miles toward Sarasota, but found nothing on their reedy shores worth shooting except eagles and cranes, but none of which were secured.

It was a godforsaken looking country too mean for a respectable 'gator to live in; or, as Charlie said, "dere warnt no land good for noffin 'cept de hummock land"; and on being asked why it was called by that name replied that he "didn't know ezactly but sposed becoz it had right smart more hummock than the pine lands." Whenever they stopped at a habitation for a drink of water, the occupying "cracker" informed them that not many 'gators were around there, but at such or such a place, a few miles away, were plenty of them. This kind of advice they followed for a better part of the day, going from one to another, until they arrived in sight of the gulf and the waning sun warned them to proceed no further. They each obtained one shot, however, Roger for the first time, and then started for town. When half way there they reached a little lake about two feet deep, and from the center of which a hundred yards distant, the eyes of a small 'gator were pointed out by Charlie; whereupon Mike alighted and fired his last two rounds. The 'gator disappearing, Charlie waded in with a stick, and reaching down into the water, pulled the 'gator ashore by the tail, with a bullet hole through its head. It was squeezed into the wagon and carried to town, where Charlie skinned it and left its beating heart on the grass. Having determined to leave that night, they cut some orange canes and gutted the market of guava jelly at twenty cents a tumbler, which was much superior to the Cuban production. They went on board the Margaret the same evening at seven, and after laying at the dock all night, bade good bye to the fish-strewn shores and the pineapple trees, and started for Tampa. During the night two women boarded the Margaret, and sitting by the door to their stateroom began to chatter and giggle; and when patience had ceased to be a virtue, Mike called to them to shut up and go to bed. They talked back, and held the door all night, even renewing the conflict the next day during the ride to Tampa—Mike accusing one of them with looking cross and making faces at him, which she indignantly denied. They arrived at Tampa at nine-thirty, and finding the invalid nearly well, expressed their canes and 'gator skin home, and prepared for their own departure.

TAMPA TO ST. AUGUSTINE.

They were roused at five o'clock on the first day of Spring, and after a late cup of coffee were driven to the depot, but the ticket agent was sleepy and only appeared as the train was about to leave, so they only secured tickets and checked their trunks at the last minute. Halting at Lakeland twenty minutes for breakfast, ten were consumed in reaching the hotel four blocks distant, and ten more in service. They were then just about to pay for the privilege of having eaten nothing when the conductor entered, to whom they attached an imaginary string and ate in peacefulness. Arriving at Ocala at one, they put up at the Ocala house, spending the afternoon in looking around town and reading late northern papers obtained at a news stand whose proprietor rejoiced in the name of "I. Dod Israel." Leaving Ocala at six, they arrived at the Silver Springs hotel about seven—a large, new, nice & comfortable house, where they enjoyed a fine supper, succeeded by singing and dancing by a couple of negro boat hands. The celebrated Silver Springs were only a few rods distant. They were about 150 feet broad with a variable depth to 70 or 80 feet, but yet so clear that a dime could have been distinctly seen upon the bottom, where the sand was free from reeds, which was the case in spots the entire nine miles to the Ocklawaha. The water was tepid and contained many fish, some appearing to be twenty inches in length, while others were shaped like arrows. The Springs were navigable for small stern wheel steamers, which reached them from Palatka by way of the St. John's and Ocklawaha rivers and the Silver Spring Run. The regular boat was the Okahumkee, on which they took their stations until the arrival of the morning train from Ocala, the passengers from which quickly crowded all the available space; whereupon, just as the lines were being cast off, and none others could make prompt-enough arrangements to follow, the Denver party stepped ashore and boarded the extra Marion, which immediately followed the Okahumkee. They had thus one little boat to themselves, with the addition of a Mrs. Zinn of Cincinnati, who had fallen into their company the preceding day; and a Mr. Wolff of New York, who was on his way to Havana. At the end of two hours, however, their number was augmented by a half dozen who had disembarked from the overcrowded Okahumkee to await the Marion. The ride down the river was delightful, the channel being very narrow, and constantly turning so that the boat frequently rubbed against the trees or banks. A few weeks later a young lady passenger was killed by a falling limb jarred from above. The forest frequently arched above the stream, and in one instance two large cypress had grown into one thirty feet from the ground, though their bases were twenty feet apart. A palmetto was also observed with a double head, while at another point the boat passed between two trees known as the cypress gates and only twenty-two feet apart. The trees were generally very tall, while underbrush, vines and water extended as far as the eye could penetrate, excepting a few small places above the water line, where leather-hued settlers were trying to raise oranges and ague. Alligators, fish, turtles and moccasins were the chief productions of the water, and a 'gator's countenance just above the line was voted to be the "nobbiest" thing in Florida. The terrapins outnumbered the Havana victorias, and as many as fifteen were counted in conference on one small log. At dark a pitch pine fire was ignited in a grate above the pilot house, the ruddy light from which illuminated the route a few rods ahead. Standing on the edge of the vessel and looking into the water, the reflection of the trees presented the appearance of sailing in the clouds. Their staterooms were small & hot, and hence they passed an uncomfortable night. At Palatka they breakfasted at the Carleton, then took the train for West Topoi, then the transfer steamer across the St. John's, and train for Augustine.

ST. AUGUSTINE.

Upon the steamer which conveyed them across the St. John's river from West Tocoi to Tokoi they met Rev. Dr. Willis Lord and wife, also headed for the Ancient City, and where they all arrived early in the forenoon. The Denver party proceeded to the Cleveland House, in the rain, but not liking its appearance, the ladies were left, while the gentlemen went prospecting. They visited every hotel in the city, including the elegant San Marco, which was full, and they finally selected the Florida, which was tolerably good with high charges. Inquiring about "bugs," the clerk said they had never had a bug in the house, and explained that during the Summer months when the hotel was closed, they permitted the large Southern spiders to accumulate, which kept the house clear of vermin. They all remained at the Florida until the 9th, during which time Roger's birthday came around again and the ladies bestowed on him some rare and costly presents, to which he responded in an eloquent speech. Rain fell the greater part of the time, but in the intervals they visited a museum where the principal stock in trade consisted of a lot of rattlesnakes killed by the cold weather, some of them being ten feet long and five inches in diameter, with fangs an inch in length. Some pelicans exhibited their voracity by catching fish on the fly, and when one attempted to swallow its food crosswise, the woman in charge reached her air down and turned the fish around. A darter bird near by, being unwilling to be outdone by a pelican, swallowed a fish of greater dimensions than its own neck. A visit to old Fort Marion and its dungeons, and the Sergeant's story of the past, were taken in as matters of course; while the Sergeant, taking in the usual fee from each, caused Mike to express a desire to resign all the places of trust and emolument held by himself and secure that of the Sergeant. The accommodations for boating were excellent, and two fishing excursions were undertaken, but the darkey sailors, who delighted in putting "Captain" on their cards, ever had ready excuses for the bad luck, with assurances of improvement the next time. The only real good luck was,

when Mike was looking another way Roger gave his line a ten pound jerk. Mike saved himself from going overboard and pulled in like he had a big one, until he felt that the fish had escaped; but he never knew what kind of a trout he had lost.

After fishing, they landed on the beach at the inlet and spent an hour in gathering shells. In their absence the "captain" had suffered the wind to drive his boat broad-

No. 78. The Boneyard, Silver Spring Creek.

No. 83. Cypress Gate, on the Ocklawaha.

side upon the beach, and on their return he was at his wit's ends. The gentlemen finally jumped the ladies aboard by taking advantage of the receding waves, and the captain and another negro, who lost his hat in the excitement, floated the boat and then sailed to the dock with the gunwale running beneath the water. On Sunday they exhibited respect for Dr. Lord by attending the Presbyterian church in expectation of hearing him preach, but he remained quiet in his pew. The customary contribution was taken at the beginning of the services, and the preacher, thinking he had made points during his sermon that had softened the hearts and pockets of his hearers, ordered a second at its close. Then he invited a Chicago Sunday School worker present to make a few remarks, which frightened those who had been shelling out for fear of a third application. After church the men visited the Dade monuments at the military cemetery, and which were low conical heaps of masonry, bearing no inscriptions. They also visited the ancient gates, and in the country beyond the city limits were entangled in a network of fences, yet succeeded in procuring a few canes for friends at home.

Homeward Bound.

Having been away two and a half months Roger felt that he could stay no longer, and accordingly Mike and Jane accompanied them to the depot at three thirty on the 9th of March, where the final goodbyes were said and the curtain dropped on their season of friendly association and enjoyment.

The travelers reached Jacksonville at dark and went to the Carleton for supper. They were cordially received and offered the proprietor two dollars for his trouble in handling their letters during their long absence, but which he declined to accept. Obtaining their sleeper tickets all right, and having just time to carry a few oranges which the market of St. Augustine did not afford, unless of frosted stock, they made close connection with the seven o'clock train. At Atlanta the next noon considerable ice was found. They patronized the buffet all day, and arriving at Cincinnati at six-fifty the next morning, took breakfast in the depot, and departed at eight-fifteen in an Ohio & M. parlor car. Rain and snow began to fall as they neared St. Louis, at which point they feared the Mississippi Pacific strike, just beginning, would delay them, but they slipped through on the Wabash all right, the Pullman representative of Truth alleging that he had only two Alton uppers at the receipt of Roger's telegram for a section. Denver parties on the car had a telegram not to start, as a snowstorm that morning had blocked all of the roads. At Kansas City the Pullman representative of Truth alleged that he had not received Roger's telegram for a center section, and there was but one remaining at each end of the car, the California cut rate having started all the millionaires and their wives and daughters in the country to seize the opportunity and save a few dollars. Col. Lessig from Florida, and Col. Raymond, from New Orleans, appeared later; and Denver was reached only an hour late on Saturday morning the 13th of March.

APPENDICES

Chronological.

Jan. 1. At St. Louis.
2. At Cincinnati.
3. "Marching through Georgia."
4. Arrival at Jacksonville.
7. Up the St. John's River.
8. Arrival at Tampa.
13. Embarked on the Mascotte.
14. At Key West.
15. Arrived at Havana.
16. Visited the Tacon theatre.
17. Dog, cock, and bullfight.
18. Riding and visited Spanish Casino.
19. At Henry Clay factory & Cervantes theatre.
20. Visited Tacon Market and sailed on harbor.
21. Dr. and Mrs. Warner called; visited Cristina market; Spangler shopping with the ladies.
22. At Captain General's Summer gardens; Dr. Wilson called in the evening.
23. At the Cabañas and Morro Castle.
24. Visited Columbus Cathedral.
25. Attended Musicale of Havana Club.
26. Visited Regla.
27. At La Punta, Campo Elysees, and Chorrera.
28. Roger held a 29 crib-hand.
30. Buying pineapple fibre handkfs.
31. At cock and bullfights with Simpson.

Feby. 1. At Castillo Principe.
2. A Holiday.
3. At the Board of Trade.
4. Mrs. Warner called in morning.
5. Pictures taken at hotel & ladies shopping with Mrs. Warner.

Feby.	6.	Went to Marianao.
	7.	Mike and ladies at church.
	8.	Went to Matanzas.
	9.	At caves of Bellamar & Chapel of Montserrat.
	10.	At the coffee plantation.
	11.	Registered for the Mascotte.
	12.	Got a doctor for Anna.
	13.	Attended lottery drawing.
	14.	Went up the river from Chorrera.
	15.	Rode to Columbus cemetery.
	16.	Mike lost his watch; went to sugar factory.
	17.	Sailed for Tampa.
	18.	Arrived at Tampa.
	22.	Sailed for Manatee.
	23.	Hunting 'gators on Manatee river.
	24.	Ditto.
	25.	Hunting at lakes toward Sarasota.
	26.	Returned to Tampa.
	27.	Had strawberries.
	28.	Met Judge Locke.
March	1.	Left Tampa for Silver Springs.
	2.	Going down the Ocklawaha.
	3.	Arrived at St. Augustine.
	4.	Visited a snake museum.
	5.	Telegraphed for money.
	6.	At Fort Marion, fishing & shelling.
	7.	Went to Presbyterian church.
	8.	Fishing.
	9.	Started home.
	10.	In Georgia.
	11.	Cincinnati to St. Louis.
	12.	Kansas City and Kansas Pacific.
	13.	Denver.

Chief Expenses

Sleeper, Denver to Kansas City	$ 8.00
Two tickets K.C. to St. Louis	15.00
Sleeper K.C. to St. Louis	4.00
Hotel, St. Louis	7.00
Two tickets S.L. to Cincinnati	20.00
Sleeper St. L. to Cincinnati	4.00
Hotel, Cincinnati	8.00
Two tickets C. to Jacksonville	46.20
Mann Sleeper C. to Jacksonville	11.00
Hotel, Jacksonville	25.15
Two tickets J. to Tampa	22.00
St. James hotel, Tampa	6.00
Palmetto House Tampa	20.00
Two tickets Tampa to Havana	35.00
San Carlos hotel Havana	182.70
Havana to Mananzas and return	15.00
San Carlos hotel at Matanzas	28.87
Havana to Tampa, 2 tickets	35.00
Trip to Manatee	20.00
Hotel at Tampa	35.12
Tampa to Ocala & Silver Springs	
Silver Springs to Palatka	12.00
Palatka to St. Augustine	1.00
Hotel at St. Augustine	40.00
St. Augustine to St. Louis	58.90
Sleepers St. Augustine to Denver	25.00
Tickets Kansas City from St. Louis	15.00

Cribbage

Mike	Roger	Mike	Roger	Mike	Roger
1.000	976	9739	9.882	18.450	18671
916	1000	990	1000	997	1000
1.000	985	1000	939	1000	965
920	1000	998	1000	897	1000
1000	921	876	1000	959	1000
925	1000	1000	880	937	1000
976	1000	1000	982	1000	824
987	1000	960	1000	980	1000
949	1000	1000	988	1000	982
966	1000	987	1000	988	1000
9.739	9.882	18.450	18.671	27.208	27.442
27.208	27.442	36.024	36.381	44.732	45.216
938	1000	940	1000	970	1000
1000	980	1000	945	1000	981
987	1000	1000	997	932	1000
975	1000*	954	1000	1000	862
1000	996	982	1000	951	1000
950	1000	1000	989	951	0000
				1000	926
995	1000	1000	904	944	1000
				1000	926
971	1000	986	1000	869	1000
				947	1000
1000	963	846	1000	983	1000
36.024	36.381	44.732	45.216	56.279	56.911

*Including a 29-hand.
Games – Mike 21. Roger 37. Total 58.
Points – 632 in favor of Roger.
Game average – Mike 970 19/58. Roger 980 7/58.